SHIFT HAPPENS

A LAYPERSONS GUIDE TO AWAKENING

written and illustrated by
GINA CHARLES

Published by Gina Charles
www.ginacharles.com
New York

Copyright © 2011 Gina Charles
All rights reserved
Published in the United States of America
Original cover design and illustrations by Gina Charles

ISBN-10: 0615485049
ISBN-13: 978-0-615-48504-1

This book was written to provide conceptual information. It is distributed with the understanding that the publisher and author are not engaged in rendering legal, medical or any other such professional services. If legal, medical or other expert assistance is required, the services of a competent professional should be sought. It is not the purpose of this book to reiterate conceptual information that is otherwise available, but instead to reintroduce it, complement and amplify it. You are encouraged to read any or all related available material, learn as much as possible, and tailor the information to your individual needs, if at all. This book contains information based on personal revelations and spiritual growth of the author, complete and as accurate as possible, and is current up to the publishing date. The purpose of this book is to present contemplative information and is at the discretion of the reader. If you do not wish to be bound by the above, you may return this book to the publisher.

For
and because of,
Anthony

The good news is, there is always good news.

CONTENTS

INTRODUCTION 7

ACKNOWLEDGEMENTS 9

PART ONE
The Bigger Picture

1. Who and Where Are We? 11
2. The Straw 17
3. Presence 20
4. Beliefs 28

PART TWO
The Three-Part Team

5. Team Me 35
6. The Software 39
7. The Pond 49
8. The Hardware 58

PART THREE
Accepting, Allowing, Attracting, Oh My

9. It's Not My Job Man 66

10 The Same Tomato 73

11. I'll Take One From Column A and Two From Column B........ 79

12. A Call To Action 84

13. Accepting, Allowing, Attracting and Doing 94

14. The Law of Attraction 98

PART FOUR
The Road Trip

15. Getting To The Shore 106

16. Sign Posts 115

17. Waking Up To The Bigger Picture 119

18. Shift Happens 123

PART FIVE
Mnemonics

Tips and Tricks to Kick Yourself Back Into Play 128

GLOSSARY 135

INTRODUCTION

The moment I acknowledged that seemingly constant, underlying feeling that something felt awry, it sparked the questions. I'm sure you're familiar with the questions I'm referring to. I bet you have asked yourself the same things. Where am I, and for that matter, who am I? In pursuit of the answers I've noticed behavior, reasoning, desire, fear and the subsequent need to control it all. It took me awhile to realize that it's not as much about discovering the best way to navigate through this human experience, as it is to just have it. More specifically, my gratitude lies in the realization that just having it, is the best way to navigate it.

I'm using my notes on this human experience to point to the shifts that usher us into living an Awakened life. It's about discovering that we are the keepers of our own happiness, and the key to our best life has been in our back pocket all along. What this book is not, is an attempt to change your mind about anything. That's your job. I can liken the writing of this book to me making you a sandwich. I can make you a sandwich, but I can't eat or digest it for you. Only you can do that. I can write the words in this book, but I can't give you Conscious expansion. The hungrier you are, the better the sandwich tastes. Spiritual growth, Conscious expansion, getting closer to God, gaining control, freeing yourself, finding your life purpose or the life of your dreams, all have the same thing in common. It's really an inside job. This is a journey for which we have shown up fully equipped. We have everything we need including the road map.

Throughout the book I use a truck load of analogies and metaphors. I believe a picture is worth a thousand words, even if your are imagining that picture in your head. Don't worry, you won't have to do all the work, I've used some actual illustrations. To paraphrase one of the best Pointers on the planet, Eckhart Tolle, I'm using words (and images) to point to the inexplicable. Associating images to information is a great way to remember stuff, and an invaluable tool to convey Truths that go beyond words. Remembering these Truths aids in reconditioning, which lends itself to Conscious expansion. Let's connect the dots and make some memorable pictures. :)

So, if you are inclined, have a seat and take a peak inside.....lol, I was talking about the book. The ambiguity was accidental.

ACKNOWLEDGEMENTS

There have been many sign posts along my path pointing me in the direction of my highest good. Recognizing them has been one of the most important steps in getting the hang of living my best life. Some of these sign posts, or pointers, came in all different shapes, sizes, and species. Some were identified as friends, others, not so much. I have learned that the biggest splinters are sometimes the best teachers. I'd like to express my acknowledgement and gratitude to them all. I thank them for their gifts, no matter how ugly or beautiful the wrapping may have been.

Now for the fun part. My deepest gratitude, love and recognition to Raul Garcia. Your love, comforting support and encouragement has been a constant in my life, including in the writing of this book. To Tyne, AKA Anthony Charles, you are my greatest gift of all. All your love, support, encouragement, patience and teachings are all icing on the cake to having you in my life. I love you beyond the words. To Heather McGrath, thank you for all of your encouragement and support not only in the writing of this book but also in life. You are the epitome of class. Big love to Emily Cardoso for the decades of unconditional love, reinforcement and laughter. You are proof there are angels among us.

My never ending love and gratitude to Theresa and Charles Casella. The warmth of your love will always be with me. To my Uncle Mikes, Michael Casella, who gave me the most precious things we have to give, his love and attention. You will be in my heart forever.

Thank you to Helaine Fuss Clendennen who is an all loving person, with the gentility and caring of a saint. You are much appreciated and loved. To Marian Minerva, thank you for your love and the late night personal bible classes way back when. Deep appreciation and admiration for teacher, friend and author, Amelia de Pazos. So much gratitude to Yvette Romano for being such a good friend even before we ever met, and ever since. Thank you to Peter Cardoso for his unconditional support. Mucho agradecimiento a Mima por todo su amor y papas fritas.

My special recognition and thanks to Natalie Zindl D'Angelo, Melina Martinez, Tina Luciano, Mary Ambrosio, Louise Spadaro, Ledgy Watkins, Christina Pagan, Melinda McGrath, Dwana Henry, and Jennifer Bailey.

PART ONE

THE BIGGER PICTURE

- 1 -
Who and Where Are We?

Who and where are we? These questions have crossed most of our minds at one time or another. We've asked ourselves these questions way back when we believed the world to be flat, and we've asked ourselves these questions when we knew the world was round. In pursuit of living my best life, I discovered where I am, and who I am.

Until I was better able to get a bird's eye view of myself and how I fit into my world, I spent a lot of time trying to make the best of this human experience. We're busy educating ourselves, pairing ourselves up, working hard, reproducing, and basically chasing our dreams. That's pretty much what it all boils down to. Aren't we all either openly searching for the life of our dreams or secretly wondering about it?

Some of us may think finding the life of our dreams comes in the way of finding a life purpose. Others may think it comes with learning how to control the experiences of our lives. Maybe some of us gave up on these notions a long time ago and are just trying to get through it. The life of my dreams is built on the knowing that I am already whole and complete, and that I am living in a benevolent construct which I call life.

Without the insight of a bigger picture, we go through the motions of our lives, doing, doing and more doing, and either forgetting to live, or ignorant to the possibility of it. No matter what your circumstance, you have everything you need to get a handle on this human experience and live an optimal life. We did not come unequipped. It's funny how on the outside we could seem different from one another, and yet still be the same all-knowing works of art on the inside. No matter where we think we are, or who we think we are, one of the things we have in common is that we all just want to be happy. If happy was buried at the bottom of a pile of junk in my closet, you'd bet I'd clean that closet out right quick.

The good news is, there is always good news. Alright, I know what you're thinking. Your mind is spewing all the "reasons" why that isn't always true. What if it is true? I haven't lived long enough to see leggings come back into fashion for nothing. I've learned a few things along the way. Two of the most important things I've learned is that most of our thoughts are not true and swimming upstream gets you nothing but tired. Simply understanding and incorporating these two concepts into your life will change your life completely. And I do mean completely. In addition, there are more concepts and practices we can use to slide over into our ideal life. If that's not good news, I don't know what is.

The good news is, there is always good news.

When I look back on some previous experiences I've had, I'm able to see good things that resulted from them. These past experiences held in them little pearls, gifts, lessons and opportunities for growth. Sometimes I was able to learn my lesson and grow from it. Other times, I was not able to accept and question my way to freedom. I didn't learn the lesson or experience the growth it would have gifted me.

Luckily our little pearls of wisdom are never lost. Those little pearls will find their way into a similar situation. They are out there patiently waiting for me. They will quite often present themselves in the form of someone or something I don't like. Someone or something I deem uncomfortable or undesirable. I now understand, these people or situations are representing an opportunity. An opportunity for me, an opportunity for growth, even though it may not look like one.

Before I recognized these situations as opportunities for growth, some of my life experiences seemed hard to understand. Life felt heavy, confusing and unfair. There were times when I believed getting to where I wanted to be would require an arduous uphill climb, and making that climb felt impossible. There were also plenty of times I did make it to the finish line, only to come up short or frazzled. It was at this point I'd find myself cursing under my breath, brushing the hair out of my eyes and smiling, as not to give anyone the idea that I wasn't in control of it all. There were, of course, some days where everything fell into place beautifully. However, because I had trouble taking the credit, I'd think the Universe/God/Source was mercifully throwing me a crumb.

I searched up, down and all around for the control panel to this ride. Eventually, I realized I hadn't looked inside. Of course! But how could I blame myself? No one ever told me to check my own pockets for what I felt I wanted and needed out of life. The very connotation of the word "need" implies there's something I don't have. I began to consider the possibility that I don't really need anything. It felt plausible to think I may already have everything I need. Up until this point I mistakenly overlooked that. Hey, I was busy. I had stuff I didn't want to do, people I didn't want to see and places I didn't want to go. Besides that, most of us grew up in cultures that taught us to look outside of ourselves for.....well, everything.. :/

Alright, onward and upward! Now we have something to work with. Let's take a look at living our best life from a different perspective. Let's approach our life with the premise that we already have everything we need for the clarity and answers to living our best lives. Our big toe is pressed right up against the starting point of our very own yellow brick road. The journey is the point. What that journey is like, how we experience our adventure, is really up to us.

We have the ability to look inside of ourselves, and use what we find to create the life of our dreams. Life itself is what we are, and the dream is where we are. That life is right now, right here, in this very moment, and in this moment, and this one. That's all we ever have. We have only, the Now.

Life itself is what we are, and
the dream is where we are.

When you fill your moment with happy, that is success. That happy successful moment will lead you to another one, and another one and before you know it, you will be the happy little camper you've always wanted to be. We have the ability to do that right now. Nothing gets off the ground until the runway is clear. Let's clear the runway.

We are powerful little pieces of the One floating around in this Universe. Or maybe it's the Universe that's floating around in us. We are already whole and complete. Sometimes we get sidetracked, we forget, we get caught up in misunderstanding and untruths - our own.

This book speaks about seeing through the misunderstanding and untruths. It speaks about who, what and where we are, and what we have to work with. It speaks about how to wake up from the unconsciousness, how to remember, and how to live an Awakened life. All the words are pointing to the same place we all long for. We are all headed toward happy. Sometimes we lose our way, and even that serves a greater purpose. Here we are, and I for one am emptying my pockets for the peaceful bliss and happiness I innately know is in there. Among a few other purposes, I came here to live happily and to have big fun. I can feel that I am heading North. I'm getting the hang of it. I'm glad I took notes along the way.

- 2 -
The Straw

When we are very young our world consists of only a few people and things. We have our parents or guardians, maybe some toys and a crib, and even a couple of little friends. That's pretty much our whole world. That's our bigger picture. As babies we become aware of our surroundings and the things in them without a formulated self-identity getting in our way. When a baby discovers an apple he/she sees it, touches it and feels it. They may smell it and maybe even unwittingly test it to see if it goes to the floor where all the other stuff goes when you throw it.

The baby does not discover the apple through the self-made identity of the thinking mind. He/she does not see the apple and judge whether it's red or fresh enough, if an orange is better, or if eating the apple will make him/her look fat in a diaper. Did you ever see a baby look into a mirror for the first time? What a trip! The discovery of "self" is a big deal, even for a baby. There's a big difference between a hand and my hand. As we grow, so usually does our world around us and our view and understanding of that world. To that we add the realization of self. Now in addition to our world and what's in it, we have the added dimension of us in our world.

I liken my world and my understanding of it to looking at life through a straw. The degree to which your Consciousness expands is equal to the degree to which the view of your world expands. Many of us live in cultures that support and foster the realization and fulfillment of self-made identities, although we may not realize it. Only upon contemplative inquiry can we find our truths. Unfortunately for us and our world, we don't practice questioning our thoughts as much as would do us good. As a result, not only are our views greatly hindered, but the expansion of our view is hindered as well. If the only thing you can see through your straw are a bunch of people running scared, you'd never know it was because a bus had careened up onto the sidewalk and was headed their way. Your view did not see the bigger picture. Without Conscious expansion, neither will you. The degree to which your Consciousness expands is the degree to which you understand yourself and the Universe.

The degree to which your Consciousness expands is the degree to which you understand yourself and the Universe.

With each expansion of Consciousness, or the growth of my understanding of ideas and concepts, the view of my bigger picture has also expanded. With each revelation or realization, my view widens and has become a panoramic scene grander than I expected. I am aware, despite the growth of the picture I see, that my bigger picture is inside the big Picture. My world is inside the Universe. I may widen and enhance the view of my bigger picture here in my world, and at the same time know there is only the one big Picture. We are all included in this Picture. This one grand Picture contains absolutely everything. It is everything. It is Consciousness, from which everything manifests.

I suspect, however, we are incapable of completely experiencing the entire big Picture while incarnate. The vastness of it all must be inscrutable to the limitations of a frontal lobe. In other words, I could never see the entire big Picture through my straw. Not to worry, we each have everything we need to do what we came here to do. We don't have to see it all to know it's there. The good news is that seeing the entire big Picture is not a prerequisite to being able to create your own heaven on earth, and to collectively create a new world.

This part of the picture, our world, is an autonomous, benevolent construct. It's all good, even if that's not what we think when we look through our straw, out into our world. This is not just a place that we have come only to Awaken from, it is a place we have come to Awaken in. Our world and where we are in it, offers us what we need at the time we need it, for the very growth that expands Consciousness, widening and enhancing our view.

I now know that the view I see through my straw-of-understanding is greatly affected by a couple of things. Firstly, acceptance of what is. Not condonation of what is, but acceptance. Secondly, awareness of the present moment, being Present as much as possible. Lastly, recognizing my own untruths, which makes all the difference. I also have the power to point my straw (my focus) on that which serves me and others. There is only one big Picture. Being here, in this place we call life, makes it seem as if there is an infinity of big, small and in between separate pieces of that one picture. This is an illusion.

- 3 -

Presence

What is the present moment? The present moment is right now. Listen. What sounds can you hear in the background of where you are right now as you read these words? Do you hear any sounds now, that you didn't notice a moment ago? Do you notice any smells or physical sensations? Notice your breathing. Can you feel your heart beating or a breeze float over your skin? These are things that are happening right now, in this present moment. They are always only happening right now in this moment. The only thing missing from the natural flow of this moment is our Attention, our Focus.

Our Attention, Awareness, Focus, Consciousness is that which we Are. We are Presence. We are Life itself. This is the true essence of who or what I am. This is the real me, Consciousness. It's you. I am referring to the essence of our true self which is thoughtless and formless. When we put our Focus on our own Awareness, or when we become aware of our own Consciousness, we are Present. We are Awake. Welcome home.

When we put our Focus on our own Awareness, or when we become aware of our own Consciousness, we are Present. We are Awake. Welcome home.

I refrain from using the term "self-realization" because I am not referring to the mind-made identity we call "me." I am not pointing to the "me" that has a name, a physical description, an occupation or defining characteristics. Nor am I referring to the term "conscious mind." We are not our minds or any part thereof. The mind is a tool that best serves that which we Are, our Consciousness, our Higher Selves. The "conscious mind" and Consciousness are two different things. The mind, described as "conscious" or not, is a tool, and is actually unconscious. We will speak more about the mind in part two. Consciousness is that which we are. It is our true self.

Upon hearing about Presence and living an Awakened life, most thinking minds, or the part of ourselves we call "me", may believe its missing something. This is natural, although the thinking mind can not understand Presence. It can comprehend a definition, however that's not the same as knowing Presence. The mind is unconscious. Presence is Conscious, or our true formless self. The unconscious mind can not exist in Presence or Consciousness, so there is no way for the mind to really know it. Unconsciousness can not exist in Consciousness. That's like trying to light a match underwater. It's not possible.

Presence is sometimes referred to as Enlightenment. He/she is Enlightened. There are many meanings for many words, each containing subjective connotations, so communicating the intangible can be tricky business. Personally I think the terms Presence, Awake, Being, and Enlightened are one and the same. I see being Present sort of like being close enough to Presence to kiss it. What bridges the gap between Present and Presence? A shift. Being Present is having your Awareness on the nowness of this present moment. It's sort of like the first step, the starting point. The recognition of the nowness of this present moment is sort of like a threshold, a portal, the door to that shift that becomes Presence, or being fused with the Now. There is also something to be said for semantics and not getting caught up in it. When you are Present or are in Presence you will know it. You will experience the shift into clarity.

Once that inner shift happens there is no mistaking it. It could be spoken about indefinitely and no matter how articulately it is expressed, it can never be completely communicated. This is because the thinking mind doesn't know Presence. It can only analytically understand the concept, but it cannot create or have the experience. The isness of it is outside the thinking mind. The mind is contained in

Presence, not the other way around. You could also describe it as the real you, Awareness or Consciousness, that is always in the background of the mind and everything we experience here in this place we call life.

How can I shift into Presence? Get Present. Place your Awareness and Focus on the present moment and what that contains. What that doesn't contain are suppositions, judgements or thoughts of the past or future. Try to empty your head of words, as best you can, even if it's intermittent. Keep going back to putting your Attention or Focus on the silence in your head. Become the Observer. Watch, so to speak, what you hear, smell, feel, sense, and most importantly, what you think. Watch your thoughts as you would a benign leaf float by in a river. Watch, notice as an observer.

Become the Observer. Watch, so to speak, what you hear, smell, feel, sense, and most importantly, what you think.

Experience this place as if you were a moviegoer seated in a theater watching a film. When you go to the movies you don't scream and cry out at the screen in protest because you are opposed or in resistance to what is happening in the movie. Why? Because you are aware the movie already is, and more importantly, you accept that. You may feel that you don't like parts of the movie, but you don't suffer to the point that it affects your life in a negative way. This is because you are the observer and believe there is no way this movie could hurt you or cause you any real suffering. Ah-Ha. This is one way to get there.

In addition to being the Observer in the present moment, you could contemplate certain concepts. Take it slow. Think about everything you experience here being in your highest good. Look around you and know that everything you see is all for you. You are loved and God or the Universe will give you what you need at the exact time you need it for your growth. I know there are times you'd swear that couldn't possibly be the case. Take a good, open-minded look at it without the pressure of thinking you have to believe it. These concepts are not things to be believed, they are things to be known. You move into them, or as your Consciousness expands you take them in, and come to know them as your truth. It is not a case of talking anyone into anything. That's not possible.

The thinking mind can speak of Presence, but it doesn't know it. It only understands it logically or intellectually. We are speaking of the inexplicable, things that are inscrutable to the thinking mind. You begin by analytically or intellectually understanding it, then you go beyond the analytical understanding of it. It's here you move into knowing. That's Conscious expansion, the Ah-Ha moment, a shift, an epiphany. You will feel it when you slide over into knowing something as your truth. You will feel the expansion, the vastness and depth of the realization. All of a sudden you have that shift and you are watching life like a movie, on the edge of your seat, with a low, constant buzz of excitement and wonder as to what will happen next.

All of a sudden you have that shift and you are watching life like a movie, on the edge of your seat, with a low, constant buzz of excitement and wonder as to what will happen next.

I used to think that once one becomes Enlightened, Present or Awakened that they're done, they did it, they made it. Of course I can't say for sure that it is not that way for some, but for the most part I don't believe it is. I don't think Enlightenment is like a line you cross into a place or a state that you don't revert back from. When you are here, incarnate, you're still using the thinking mind to function in this place. You are still susceptible to the mind, so to speak. Your mind still thinks thoughts. The thoughts aren't true. That's just the nature of the mind. Birds fly, fish swim, minds think. The good news is that the Present, Awakened person's mind gets reconditioned, or trained. It functions a little differently, more peacefully and happily than it did before. All the time we spend practicing complaining and the rotten emotions we feel because of it is conditioning the brain as well. This type of behavior conditions the brain to fire off "negative" and uncomfortable responses. Finding the peace and clarity in Presence reprograms those "negative" responses and in addition creates new positive responses and triggers.

The reason you don't see spiritual teachers who are Present or Awakened fist fighting with someone who just took

25

their parking space is because they have come to know, see and process things differently. Everything happens for me. They know this. That's not to say for a brief moment they don't feel slighted or even a bit angry. They can. The difference is they immediately notice the anger, like an observer, and see right through it. They are not consumed by it and they don't go unconscious in it. They stay present. "Oh look, my thinking mind believed something so much that when it did not happen, it became angry. Look at that." It's like watching a movie and noticing how angry one of the characters become. You may empathize with the anger that the character is feeling and exhibiting in the movie, but you don't empathize with it so much so that you become unconscious in it and begin to beat up the person seated next to you. At least I hope not. :/ You are the Observer.

One of the results of living as a Present Observer are the moments we bridge that gap between Present and Presence. This is where we shift into meshing with the Now, and experience what is referred to as Satori, or Kensho. Both these terms are often used interchangeably. They roughly translate to moments of Enlightenment. Some of us may experience events that thrust us into living in Presence. I'm guessing these people are few and far between. For others, moving into living a life of Presence is more of a journey. You have moments of Satori, or brief moments of Enlightenment, where you expand into the vast depth and knowingness of the Now. It happens intermittently. It could happen while riding in the passenger seat of a car, looking out the window, watching this place like a movie.

How does that happen? I become Aware or Present. My focus is on the present moment and all that the present moment holds. I notice my surroundings, what I see, hear, and feel without the inner chatter in my head. Behind the silence in my mind there is a knowing that everything I see is all for me. I am that loved. I am that important. I already have everything I need. Everything is in the exact place it should be at the exact time it's supposed to be. I have discovered that silently being aware of all of this while being Present, are the ingredients for the recipe for that shift. I have experienced this as a portal to that shift, or that sliding over into the hugeness of meshing with Now.

Once you slide over into that space, everything seems different. You have no idea what will happen in this moment and that is accompanied by an underlying low buzz of excitement rather than the anxiety of not knowing. You readily and automatically accept the not knowing and embrace it as the gift it is. That embrace flowers into the low, steady buzz of elation. The next moment comes and you feel the same way, and the next. You expand. It feels like the innocent wonder and excitement of a child being handed one birthday gift after another. Of course these are words, and the best I can do to point to the inexplicable. Suffice it to say, it's like nothing else you've ever experienced.

It feels like the innocent wonder and excitement
of a child being handed one birthday gift after another.

- 4 -

Beliefs

The thinking mind can rapid-fire a multitude of reasons why it believes it needs to live an Awakened life. It may even try to talk itself into believing it has already "accomplished" it. All of this is natural behavior for the mind, although none of it is true. In Presence, none of those thoughts can exist anyway. The mind is not who we are. The mind is a tool, a very powerful and valuable tool. It is not that which we are, or our true Self. The mind is unconsciousness, and Consciousness is our true formless self. Nevertheless, the mind is only doing what it does, producing thoughts and creating beliefs.

The mind produces thoughts, called "reasons", as proof to validate or confirm the original thought. Once the mind has produced the thought and deduced enough validating reasons around it, it packs it all up into what we call beliefs. Unfortunately we don't always remember to question our thoughts and beliefs. However, luckily for us, we do possess the ability to do that. We can question what our minds say before we dive into believing it. Through inquiry we have the ability to see through our untrue thoughts, and thus free ourselves from being submersed in the unconsciousness of the thinking mind. We are able to free ourselves from the pain and suffering. We are able to avoid experiencing the pain and suffering in the first place. It's like being handcuffed and then realizing the key to those handcuffs was in the palm of our hand the whole time. We just forgot we had the key.

Through inquiry we have the ability to see through our untrue thoughts, and thus free ourselves from being submersed in the unconsciousness of the thinking mind.

One of my first clues that I am having an untrue, fear-based thought is that these types of thoughts don't feel good. They make me feel anxious, pressured, fearful, overwhelmed and any other "negative" feeling I may have. I have skipped right over recognizing my body sounding the feel-bad alarm, as a result of believing an untrue thought. Those very feelings of anxiety, overwhelm, and every other bad feeling, were in and of themselves alarms and sign posts. They were the sign posts that I zoomed right past while continuing to believe one unquestioned thought after the other. In addition to feeling bad, I was also veering off the path of my best life. I rode my mistaken beliefs onto the off ramp and sped along as my highest good tried to flag me down. :/

Thoughts, related in some way, when packed up together form a belief. Sort of like a snow ball. A snowball is made out of a bunch of snowflakes. A belief is made out of a bunch of thoughts. A lot of us create one little snow ball after the other. We do this so automatically that we hardly ever take the time to examine the thought flakes that go into creating a belief.

What a tangled web we weave, when first we practice to believe. We wonder why things feel so difficult, meanwhile we're standing there bogged down with an armful of cold, cumbersome little snow balls and a growing case of frost bite. One untrue, unexamined thought attracts another one. Before long we find ourselves at war, slinging snowballs at ourselves and each other.

What a tangled web we weave,
when first we practice to believe.

With this understanding it's easier to get a birds eye view of how we arrive at what we may refer to as life turbulence. We have thoughts. We don't question them. Some of these thoughts hitch themselves up with like thoughts and become our beliefs. It can be life changing to realize that some of our most fervent convictions may have been built on misleading fallacies. Realizing this would be a shift into freedom. This is a most empowering place to be. Not only do you experience the succulence of freedom, but you clear your own runway and give yourself the ability to soar to new heights.

Beliefs are very powerful things. They have the power to steer our lives in one direction, or in an entirely different direction. The thought of traveling in the opposite direction of my highest good would certainly explain the times when life felt difficult and disappointing. Having difficult life experiences are directly linked to believing untrue thoughts. These very unquestioned thoughts get packaged into ill-fated beliefs. Wars, between ourselves and whole nations, are fought on beliefs.

Having difficult life experiences are
directly linked to believing untrue thoughts.

My mind cringed at the supposition of how much time and energy I may have wasted digging my heels into what I now realize were only illusions. These unfounded beliefs became the very cracked foundation upon which I had built major portions of my life. This was huge for me. Realizing I may have been navigating my life based on untruths felt like a rug being pulled out from under me. That only lasted a second, because my mind quickly connected the dots on how having a bogus map may be the very reason I didn't always find the pot of gold. Okay, so my mistaken beliefs served as sort of a broken compass, or a bogus map. This, of course, led me a tad bit off the path of my highest good where I wondered where I had gone wrong and why everything seemed so difficult.

Having this thought about wasting my time and energy believing untruths makes me feel bad. Because I feel bad when I have that thought, I recognize this as an untruth as well. Seems a bit confusing, but it's not. It's always simple, although not always easy. We have the simple concept of feeling bad when we have an untrue thought. The concept adds that the bad feeling I experience serves as an alarm that sounds in my body to let me know when I'm believing an untruth. Recognizing the Truth is enough. I get a bad feeling when I have an untrue thought or belief. Recognizing this helps me to dismiss my mistaken beliefs, and touch base with my true self. Even if I'm unable to see where my belief is untrue, I still have the understanding that it could be. That alone can make a huge difference.

Once I recognize a feel-bad thought or belief, how do I question it? Identify what your thought or belief is in a simple statement. "I've wasted so much of my time!" Is that absolutely true? "Yes!" Do you know for sure that you wasted your time? "Well, yes." Are you positive that you did not learn something of value along the way? "Uh, well...no, I can't be positive about that." Do you know for sure that nothing positive came out of it for yourself or for others? "No." So is it absolutely true that you wasted your time? "No." You really can't be certain that you did not learn or accomplish something that will be of value to you at some point. You really have no way of knowing that nothing at all positive will come out of it. So right then and there I can recognize the statement, "I've wasted so much of my time" as an untruth. It's a lie. When I'm able to recognize a statement as being untrue, there's no way I can suffer. It's not possible. What's the opposite of "I've wasted so much of my time!"? I did not waste so much of my time.

When I'm able to recognize a statement as
being untrue, there's no way I can suffer.

No time is ever wasted. Everything that happens is for a reason. What comes my way is always for my good and at the perfect moment. In that there are the opportunities, when accepted, that gift me growth. Feeling bad, because of believing an unquestioned thought, is the Universe's way of tapping us on the shoulder. It's a little tap to wake us up. It's a reminder that we have fallen asleep at the wheel. We're unconscious. It serves as a sign post that we are not Present in the moment. We have forgotten that everything is for us, and everything is as it should be. Sometimes we don't feel that tap on our shoulder, so the Universe may give us a slap on the back. We don't always acknowledge that either. This could go on and on until we reach a point in our lives where we feel ineffective or stagnated. This is the place we feel exhausted, disappointed or outright unhappy.

Well then, what am I supposed to believe? Nothing. There isn't anything to believe. There is no such thing as should. "I really should push myself to climb the ladder at my job." Is that absolutely true? No. I have no way of knowing if pushing myself is in my best interest. I don't know that if I gave in to my underlying feeling of wanting to quit, that it wouldn't lead me to the career of my dreams. So is it true that you should push yourself into the very direction you obviously don't want to be going? No.

The mind believes there are things to be believed. That's because the mind, as well meaning as it sometimes is, does not understand the clarity of Consciousness. In Consciousness there is a clarity of knowing. That is very different from a set of beliefs. If you stray from those beliefs it is implied you will get undesired results. It is implied you have done something wrong. That's not possible. Whatever results we get from our actions or beliefs are the perfect results we need for our growth, freedom and empowerment at the precise moment we need them. Our experiences, what comes our way, is always in our highest good. It is when we believe things are not as they should be that we suffer. How do I recognize the difference? Question your thoughts. The Work of Byron Katie is an invaluable and simple process in questioning thought. Her process is available on her website. Thank you Katie. :)

We all have fear-based, untrue thoughts and hold mistaken beliefs from time to time. That's natural and common, but we don't have to believe them. The good news is, and this may be some of the best news we'll ever hear, we are capable of seeing through these untruths. Our freedom lies in doing so. We've been wearing the ruby slippers all along.

And in this very moment you are exactly how and where you are supposed to be. :)

PART TWO

THE THREE-PART TEAM

- 5 -
Team Me

I already have everything I need to live my best life. So, what exactly are these things that I have and where am I keeping all this stuff? If I already have everything I need, then the idea of searching for anything outside of myself would seem silly. In pursuit of a happy life, I decided to follow my gut.....well, into my gut. I would take the natural journey inward. In doing so I discovered seemingly arbitrary realizations. I also learned that nothing is arbitrary. Although we possess free will, which could translate as random personal whim, every part of ourselves and our experiences here are deliberate and purposeful. Not recognizing this colossal collaboration doesn't change it.

Over the years I've read a bunch of books, listened to CDs, MP3s, and watched DVDs. I filled notebooks with written exercises, tried different meditations and learned tips, tricks, techniques and concepts on things spiritual and metaphysical. When I read what Echkart Tolle wrote about words being pointers to the inexplicable, it led me to seeing a bird's eye view of all my reading, writing and contemplating.

All of these mediums of information weren't just talking about indiscriminate self-growth. Collectively, this body of information was full of sign posts. They were also all pointing in the same direction. All rays lead to the sun, as the saying goes. Why? What does the sun represent? The sun represents Source. We are the Source. The rays we follow to the Sun are our own realizations, our Ah-Ha moments that are Conscious expansion, or spiritual growth.

With each revelation or realization I experienced, I got a little closer to the Sun. I didn't realize this at that time, but in retrospect, I can see that's what was happening. At the same time, coming closer to the Sun resulted in the clearing of my own runway. Little by little, I was sweeping up and throwing out the garbage. I was recognizing and discarding attachment, untrue thoughts and beliefs, and learning acceptance. By clearing away stuff I never needed, I found where everything I already had was. In other words, here in this life, my Higher Self is like a well. My abundant, everlasting well of Source. A well only I can find and only I can drink from.

> By clearing away stuff I never needed,
> I found where everything I already had was.

I am my Higher Self, Consciousness. I am here in this construct we refer to as life, riding around in the vehicle I call my body, with the help of my thinking mind who calls itself "me." Of course, being in a body and using the thinking mind leaves me open to occasional unconsciousness. That's when I forget. I momentarily forget about my well of Source and the present moment. I get caught up in my stories about how things are, which is inevitably followed by stories about how things should be. I momentarily lose the bigger picture and believe my thoughts without questioning them. Inevitably I suffer to some degree.

When I recognize the discomfort of this momentary lapse, I step into the present moment, and I am Awake. I hear my thoughts, watch them as an observer, and question them. I drink from my own well and anything unpleasant falls away. I remember who I am and what I'm working with. I'm working with a body, a mind, and Source.

One day, while explaining this three-part concept to my son Anthony, he offered an analogy that I feel accurately represents the three-part team in a timely, relevant way: The body is the hardware, the computer itself. The brain is the software, the operating system that runs the computer. The electricity is that which I Am, the real me. This is a very pertinent representation. The computer does what the software programs it to do. You can install and uninstall different programs. There are programs running in the background. Without the electricity, the software and computer don't work at all. Yes, an applicable parallel for the new millennium.

The body is the hardware, the computer itself. The brain is the software, the operating system that runs the computer. The electricity is that which I Am, the real me.

This three-part team is separately like three puzzle pieces that fit together perfectly. The thinking mind is essential. It's potential is limitless. Then, there's the body, my vehicle, the other team member whom I have relied on for so much. This team member I ran ragged, pushed too far and didn't listen to on so many occasions. Finally, there's my Higher Self, who knows what I need, when I need it, and where to find it. There we were, my Higher Self, my thinking mind and my body. The Captain, the co-pilot and the vessel. Now we're going places.

The Software

The thinking mind creates, makes or breaks how we interpret our experiences here. It uses judgements, labels and past experiences as filters to do this. Logic is the guise under which it deliberates, although when closely examined, is often the very thing that it lacks. Nevertheless, it's complexity and unbound potential is unsurpassed. It's not like just any computer, it's the most powerful, complex computer on the planet. If that wasn't impressive enough, it also gets us to believe almost everything it says. Let me word that more accurately, it gets itself to believe almost everything it says. By stringing together thoughts, it creates beliefs. These thoughts and subsequent beliefs produce feelings and emotions in the body. The thinking mind produces thoughts and beliefs that self-serve a specific end. Unconscious thought serves unconscious beliefs.

If, for example I held the unconscious belief that I was worthless, my thoughts would reflect that belief. These thoughts forge choices and decisions in our lives. This is the case whether or not I'm aware of it. In other words, in believing myself to be worthless, I would have thoughts that ultimately make other things and people more important than me. When the pain of self-disregard surfaces we become angry. Part of the problem is that we don't recognize it as self-disregard. We mistakenly believe the problem is caused by someone or something outside of ourselves. Self-disregard will invite feelings of inferiority and unimportance. The problem or situation we experience will induce those same feelings that come from believing ourselves worthless.

These uncomfortable situations will continue to occur in our experiences, creating patterns, until or unless we get the message that we are believing an untruth. Often our anger is projected outward because it's too painful to realize that it is ourselves that we are really angry with. If I sacrifice what's in my highest good, to accommodate someone or something else because of believing the lie of worthlessness, I suffer. Who believed the lie? Me. Who, in the situation, treated me as unworthy first? Me. It was all me. My thoughts reflected my belief of unworthiness. We have pain and suffering when we believe any untruth. This is good news. Yes, good news. This pain or discomfort serves as our personal, loving tap on the shoulder. It's a sign post, pointing to a lie. :)

These uncomfortable situations will continue to occur in our experiences, creating patterns, until or unless we get the message that we are believing an untruth.

For a time I pondered the thinking mind. Why is it so hard to understand? Why does it spew lies and talk incessantly? After asking these questions, I became suspect of the mind. Well, maybe not the entire thing, but at least the frontal lobe. Thought to be the most recently evolved part of the cortex, the neocortex is the part of the brain that's celebrated as what separates us from other living creatures. This is the part of the brain that is capable of the sometimes fallaciously acclaimed logic and reason, the very reason we mistakingly believe we are superior.

For me, this is a monumental example of the pain and suffering created out of believing untruths. Believing the untruth that humans are superior to other living creatures, as well as superior to one another, has caused egregious pain and suffering in our world. Atrocities committed not only on each other, but to other living creatures as well. Every time we lack respect for Life in any form, we lack respect for ourselves. Every time we meet life with unkindness, we meet ourselves with the same. The outside reflects the inside. The degree to which you are hurtful to other living creatures, is in direct proportion to how hurtful you are to yourself. This is also indicative of the regard in which you hold yourself. We are Life itself. Those with respect for life, respect themselves. Holding ourselves or others in less than the highest regard and respect is the painful result of believing untruths.

We are a curious species that in direct irony to our "superior" ability to reason, can't seem to find a way to live as peacefully as "lesser evolved" creatures. These thoughts led me to wondering if the thinking mind wasn't something we were supposed to evolve out of. Were we supposed to find a way to go beyond it, and thereby eradicate this deviser of war and suffering? I was reluctantly starting to feel like the thinking mind, this software, was my enemy. .....But that didn't feel right either. Of course there is another side to this coin as well. On that side, there is empathy, caring, generosity, peace, and the list goes on and on. There are so many people on the planet who are living in peace with themselves, others and their environment. They are out there shining their light into the world. They are using their minds to better their lives, and the lives of others. Certainly, the thinking mind is an amazingly powerful tool.

There are so many people on the planet who are living in peace with themselves, others and their environment. They are out there shining their light into the world.

"Ah-Ha! The thinking mind is my friend after all! What a relief!" Hey, wait, not so fast. It may be your friend but remember it will not pass up the chance to grab the steering wheel, cut hard and fast to the left and floor it into rough terrain. It likes it's job, thinking, thinking and more thinking, and it wants to do it as much as possible. It can start off as slow and easy as a train just beginning to move it's wheels on the track. The mind has a thought and almost as immediately it assigns meaning to it. "Should I go to the party?" The thinking mind begins to scan and examine that thought. "Well, if I go I'll have to go alone and people will know I'm no longer in a relationship." The wheels of the train begin to turn and the train slowly starts to move forward. "They may think my partner left me." The infusion of a fear-based thought gives way to subsequent emotion, which lends itself to the attraction of more of the same.

The train starts to pick up some speed. "What will I say when they ask me?" The mind deliberates, ruminates and chews on several possibilities. "I'll just say it was mutual." Now the train is off and running. It's gliding quickly along on the track. "What am I going to wear? If I wear this I'll look like.....and if I wear that I'll look like......and they'll think....." Now the train is darting full speed ahead. "......And then I'll say.....because I remember what happened the last time.....and there's no way I'm going to......" When the mind is unconsciously submersed in unquestioned thought, it's similar to being on a train that's traveling so fast, that the outside scenery (Reality) is blurred.

When the mind is unconsciously submersed in unquestioned thought, it's similar to being on a train that's traveling so fast, that the outside scenery (Reality) is blurred.

The careening cabin begins to shake but the mind is so unconscious in thought that it doesn't even notice. Welcome! You are aboard the Crazy Train! Needless to say this is not a pleasant experience. Sometimes we don't even realize we're hurtling unconsciously on the Crazy Train, so we can't make

an effort to slow the train down in an attempt to stop it. Sometimes we just hop from car to car completely absorbed in our stories and sermonizing on about one subject or another. It doesn't matter what the topic is as long as the mind gets to drone on. The mind unconsciously speechifies in total belief of it's every word, instead of observing and realizing what's actually happening.

The mind is so clever that it even gets us to believe that our discomfort is caused by someone or something else. No one has that kind of power over us, but if we wake up to realize this, then the thinking parade would be over. Ending the thinking parade is the last thing the mind wants to happen. It's no wonder we feel tense, anxious, pressured, fearful or just plain wiped out. I'm tired just from talking about it. Realize when you're on the Crazy Train. Then get the hell off. Jump if you have to. How? Get Present. Getting Present is the equivalent of pulling the emergency brake.

Getting Present is the equivalent of
pulling the emergency brake.

So how do we work with the thinking mind? It works well for me when I think of the mind like a small child that needs a lot of attention. A small child's emotions can swing, like a pendulum, from one side to the other. Sometimes kids, even some grown-ups, don't care whether they get good attention or bad attention, as long as they get some attention. It's helpful, when the mind rapid-fires fear-based thoughts, to just pat it on the head, thank it, and tell it to run along. If a small child ran up to me and said, "If you don't give me a lollypop your head is gonna blow off and roll away!", I probably would not grab hold of my head and run screaming. I'd probably say something more like, "Yea, okay kid. Now run along, you're bothering me."

I recognize, that although nothing is impossible, I really have no way of knowing if my head actually is going to blow off and roll away. There is no guarantee that this will definitely happen. This means that it is not absolutely true. Since it is not absolutely true, why on earth would I get my knickers in a bunch about it? I wouldn't. I realize this and see through it.

Noticing and reacting to my thoughts in this way is freeing and empowering.

The heart beats, rain falls down and the mind thinks. That's what it does. That's what it's supposed to do. When it rains, it rains. It doesn't just rain over here because the ground is dry, and not over there because the ground is already damp. It just rains. Sometimes the mind chatters away unremittingly about anything and everything. The thinking mind speaks of things past, present, and things that are nothing but imaginary, as the future is not happening now. Some of these thoughts produce feelings of discomfort, hence the tip-off that we are believing a lie.

The mind loves drama. In an attempt to better ourselves and our lives we allow the mind to think, think, think up all the things we could, should and would do, do, do. We look for things to alleviate the seemingly unrelenting rants. Craving quiet and stillness is innate even though the mind is usually speaking over it. We welcome those moments when the white waters of our thinking settle down and we allow ourselves to float along peacefully. Thank goodness for that, because before long we are back to work making genuine efforts to steer our ship in another guesstimated direction.

What if I don't make the right choices? How do I know what the right choices are? Here we are again, right back to square one. Swing your partner, dosey doe! You get the picture. Here we are again thinking, thinking, thinking. The mind will never miss a chance to leap into action, take control and lead the thinking parade, no matter where it leads. Don't be fooled to think your thinking is really in your best interest. Its desire is simply to do what it does, think.

We all have the same software. We all think unconsciously. What's a thinking mind to do? There must be a way to think without the inevitability of veering off my path. The good news is, there is a way. Thinking is in my best interest when I am Present, Conscious, Aware. Conscious thinking is the kind of thinking the mind was meant to do. This was the kind of thinking the mind probably used to do before it discovered itself, gave itself a name, dressed itself up and promoted itself to Captain.

Thinking is in my best interest when
I am Present, Conscious, Aware.

I eventually realized that the thinking mind is like a tool. A tool that we use, or a tool that uses us. The mind is a helper, an assistant, a co-pilot of sorts. I believe this is how the thinking mind is meant to be used, or could best be used. If it would just follow the directions of my inner compass, instead of trying to get anywhere with no real sense of direction, it would be a smooth ride. My Higher Self holds the compass. My inner compass is always pointed toward my highest good, self-growth, my life purpose or the life of my dreams. It makes perfect sense for my thinking mind to follow my inner GPS. Regardless of what kind of perfect sense it made, I could feel that my thinking mind wasn't feelin' it. It did not like the idea of taking direction from anyone...anywhere....anytime.

However, I could not deny that a smooth ride did seem rather appealing. I let it stew for awhile and then came up with what turned out to be a good idea, a compromise, a deal. That seemed only fair.

If my thinking mind would make an effort to create a habit of checking in with the Captain, my Higher Self, for directions, the ride would be so much smoother and more enjoyable. The ride would not only be smooth and enjoyable, but get this - a thinking mind loves this - my mind could have all the credit for it! My thinking mind could have all the credit for every good thing that comes my way. It could claim responsibility, based on its ingenuity, for the subsequent fulfillment and happiness I experience. (Technically, that would be true. My mind would be ingenious if it checked the inner compass!)

My thinking mind was so happy! It loved that idea and was satisfied to believe that without itself, this idea could never even have happened in the first place. It ripped off it's hat and descended into a deep and emotional bow. I heard, "Bravo!" being yelled in the background. That happens to still be the very word I hear my thinking mind shout when anything goes well for me. It takes all the credit and everything else but the blame. This gives me a warm, happy feeling in the belly which tells me the Captain is happy to give the co-pilot all the credit. After all, a deal's a deal.

The Pond

Complex as the thinking mind can be, an image is sometimes just the container that helps us see all the little pieces at once. In this case the image is a pond. I know, it seems too serene to encompass some of the chaos of the mind, but it works. It gave me a concise perspective of the difference between living an Awakened, Present, Conscious life, and not.

When I came to realize the difference between living Consciously and unconsciously, I realized that my thinking mind hadn't gotten the bigger picture. Understanding this was especially helpful for me because while I was so busy doing, doing, doing, I never even saw myself veering off into an unhappy place.

I couldn't understand how I got to an unhappy place after all my good intentions and hard work. This often led to an exhausting downward spiral of pushing even harder in response to undesirable results. We all know where this kind of spiral leads. It often led me to finding myself face down on the floor with nothing to show for my hard work. If that wasn't frustrating enough, I knew I must be missing something, but I just didn't know what it was, where it was, or how to get to it. :/

Understanding the difference between living Consciously and unconsciously made all the difference for me. While speaking about this realization in a phone conversation one day, it came out of my mouth as an analogy of a pond. My friend was able to understand the concept behind the analogy, and later told me she found it very helpful. It helped her to become aware of when she was swimming into troubled waters.

I've designated three areas of the pond. There is the inner circle, the outer circle, and the shore. The inner circle contains the dark, cold, feel-bad waters. This is not a good swim, and when we are there we really don't want to be. The inner circle is filled with life events we label "bad" or "painful."

The outer circle of the pond contains the clear, warm, feel-good water. This is where we all want to be. The outer circle of the pond is filled with life events we label "good" or "happy." Both the inner and outer circles represent the thinking mind.

Lastly, there's the shore. The shore is Consciousness. It is where we find our abundant, everlasting well of Source. It is where your Higher Self/Soul is holding the compass to your best life.

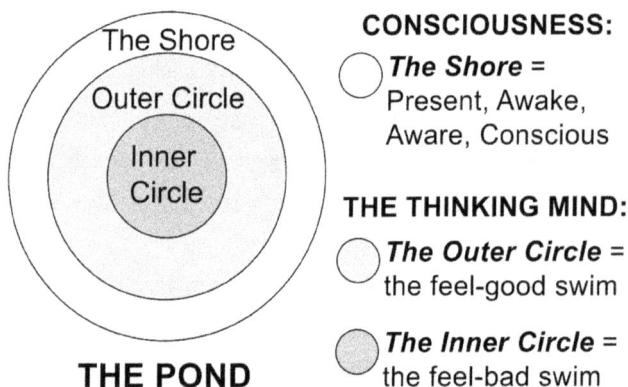

THE POND

CONSCIOUSNESS:
The Shore =
Present, Awake,
Aware, Conscious

THE THINKING MIND:
The Outer Circle =
the feel-good swim

The Inner Circle =
the feel-bad swim

When we are in the pond, we are in our thinking minds. We are absorbed into our stories, into our circumstances, and the meanings and labels we create around them. We are unaware and outside of the present moment. We are unconscious. We believe almost anything our minds are thinking, true or not. We identify with the self-made identity and believe that's who we are. Sometimes we float off into the feel-bad waters of the inner circle and splash around trying to find our way back. Other times we're splashing around in the outer circle enjoying a swim in the feel-good waters. Either way, we're still in the pond, splashing around.

We have no idea there is anything more, anything different, anything better than the outer feel-good ring. We don't realize there is a shore. If we don't realize there is a shore (Consciousness) we spend our lives swimming back and forth between the feel-bad and the feel-good side of life. It's from here the thinking mind takes it's best guess at what and where our best life may be. And 'round and 'round we go.

If we don't realize there is a shore (Consciousness)
we spend our lives swimming back and forth
between the feel-bad and the feel-good side of life.

Even those of us that consider ourselves living a happy and fulfilled life still experience some degree of choppy water from time to time. In pursuit of good and wonderful things we can still find ourselves floundering. My hard and fast swimming took the form of reading books, going to seminars, making lists, workout regimens, education and the popular positive thinking. These and many more endeavors were in lieu of enjoying the feel-good waters. I experienced successes here and there. It was all good until something happened, or didn't happen, the way I thought it should. That could have been anything from losing a job to getting rain on my new boots.

Anything I deemed unacceptable, is what I immediately resisted. While being in resistance to what was, and believing my own untruths, I would sometimes continue to swim so hard to reach that happy outer circle, that I'd wear myself out. Despite making headway into the clear waters of the outer ring, I inevitably ended up doggie paddling frantically just to stay afloat. Before I knew it I was right back in the cold, murky water. I hardly ever allowed myself to just float. Floating was for wussies. Floating was for people that didn't take life by the horns and make good things happen for themselves. Floating was for quitters. Lie, lie and lie. The trouble is, I believed them all.

Two of the fastest ways back to my yucky inner circle was non-acceptance, and believing my own lies. Nothing like a little resistance and gullibility to veer me off into the feel-bad waters. Simply put, this is unconscious living. Before long I'd muster up enough drive to attempt another swim back to the outer, happy ring. Regardless of which direction I was headed, I would sometimes find myself swimming in circles, full speed ahead. There I was, making no headway at all, just splashing around and trying not to drown. I felt the struggle and swam even harder. Why would I have to struggle so much? This was not supposed to happen. I worked very hard. I applied concentrated effort. When people work hard and make an effort they are supposed to reap good benefits. It's supposed to make things better and easier, not harder. Again, the problem was that I believed all of these thoughts.

Inside every hot bag of poop is a pearl. Well, it's nice to know that within every "problem" comes something of value, a pearl of wisdom to grow by. Sometimes there's more than one pearl of wisdom to be had. I can't say exactly how many times I had this particular hot bag of poop in my hands and never reached inside to find my pearls, my gifts, my lessons. If everything happens for a reason, what's the reason for my pattern of working so hard and not achieving the results I wanted? Maybe those results were not in my highest good. Maybe I only thought they were. :/

Inside every hot bag of poop is a pearl.

I realized there's just no way I could compare the imagination of the Universe or God to the small percentage of my miniscule brain that is my imagination. In other words, why would I think my thinking mind could single-handedly conjure up the right people, situations and things, at the exact right time, to create everything for my highest good? Not only that, but do it all in an easy, effortless and enjoyable way. The chances of my thinking mind being able to do that at this point in human evolution are pretty much nonexistent. I would bet the Universe's capability to conjure up the right person, situation or thing at the exact perfect moment, all in line with my highest good, consistently, is far greater than my thinking mind's capability to do that. This realization was my first pearl.

Turns out there was another pearl in that hot bag of stank. You never have to swim so hard that you feel like you're drowning. If you do, you're doing it wrong (unconsciously.) If you feel bad, drained, spent, a little turned off or just plain horrible, these are signs you're headed into muddy waters. They are symptoms of unconsciousness. The uncomfortable symptoms themselves are sign posts or messages pointing to the fact you are headed into painful waters. The point of the pointing, is pointing to our momentary lapse into unconsciousness. We are believing untruths and/or we are in resistance to what is.

So what can I do? Float. Yet another pearl. Stop splashing around. Quit it. When I felt overwhelmed, stagnated, spent or just plain bad, I stopped all that splashing around. I stopped the relentless inner rant. I stopped the struggle, took a breath and floated. Accept, not condone, what already is. No matter what it is. I floated in silence. I observed my thinking mind almost as if I were standing beside it. I stopped believing every thought and began questioning them. I practiced "no mind", a Buddhist term basically meaning turning off the volume in the head. I came to know the peace of silence, even if only intermittently. Sometimes I was inspired to swim, and I did, but only when I felt inspired to do so. I did not swim just because my thinking mind spewed reasons why I should be swimming. Before long, I found myself touching the shore.

I learned that no matter how good I may have gotten at getting into the feel-good waters of the pond, I was still in the pond. That side or this side, I'm still in the pond, still inside my thinking mind. The point is to get out of the pond. Get out and up onto the shore of Consciousness where I am Awake and

Aware. It's from here I can dive back in at any time and enjoy the water no matter where in the pond I am. While Conscious, I can use and observe the mind without falling into it and submersing myself in its unconsciousness. When Presence is in the pond, the thinking mind quietly takes it's first mate position. It automatically falls into its ideal, optimal function, serving Consciousness.

While Conscious, I can use and observe the mind without falling into it and submersing myself in its unconsciousness.

I may lapse back into non-acceptance or believing some of my own untruths, but eventually I remember. I notice I was asleep and I wake up. If I find myself painfully splashing around I realize that I'm in resistance, or trying too hard, no doubt from believing my own lies. So I stop struggling and I float. I get Present. Now I can have some fun. Not the kind of volatile, dependent fun that is attached to a self-created identity. I can have Awakened fun. This kind of fun and enjoyment is independently fulfilling and enhances the swim without veering me off course.

It's paradoxical, ironic, and weird. The very tool we have to rewire, observe, enhance or wake up from the thinking mind, is the thinking mind! That thought creates the kind of weirdness you feel when looking into the never ending reflection of two mirrors. It's also kind of like a surgeon operating on herself. The good news is, the thinking mind can do that. If the thinking mind believes it's walking toward it's own demise, it will dig in its heels and fight an uncomfortable fight. At least that's been my experience. But, if it understands what an imperative part of the team it is, why wouldn't it comply? It's not trying to be eradicated.

By falling into it's rightful place on the team, the thinking mind would be enhanced and valued even more. All the mind has to do is secretly check the map. Yes, it would have to give up leading the unconscious ranting parade it loves so much, but the mind would be trading it for always doing the right thing at the right time. This kind of illustrious prowess and artistry can only be met with the deepest gratitude and admiration. Hmmm....which is better, droning on unconsciously just for the pleasure of leading the ranting parade, or being exalted to Grand Poobah of the parade? Now that's a choice the thinking mind can really chew on.

Unconsciousness comes in different forms. There are thinking minds out there that live for the scrutiny of it all, marching to the beat of positivity, and others that just love the constant negative bitch-fest. Either way, there is such a thing as a thinking addiction. The mind has it's sly little hands wrapped so tightly around the steering wheel it would just as soon fist fight you than let it go. The mind will not easily give up its control. Noticing this behavior brings you into the present moment, which causes the mind to quickly and automatically let go of the wheel. Yes, the mind is a surgeon that can successfully operate on itself. Our Focus is the magic wand and we always have free will as to where to point it. For sure, the thinking mind is an amazing, admired and valuable part of the team. :)

Our Focus is the magic wand and we
always have free will as to where to point it.

- 8 -

The Hardware

The Hardware is the vehicle, the form, the body, in which we get around in this place. It's a miraculous creation. Outside of a little maintenance, it's pretty autonomous. I mean, we're not doing any breathing as much as we're experiencing the body breathing. We're not doing any digesting, or sloughing off of old cells, or actually pumping any blood. The body has all that covered. Thank goodness for that because I'd never be able to do any of that, and....well, anything else.

Our bodies house messages in the form of feelings and emotions. These feelings and emotions are sign posts. Through good feelings and emotions we can be guided to move toward our higher good. Some feelings and emotions are considered painful. Our brain sometimes considers painful emotions dangerous and prompts us to push them away. Practicing silently connecting with our physiological feelings and emotions is one of the most powerful practices we can implement.

Our bodies house messages in
the form of feelings and emotions.

When I'm under pressure or other strong uncomfortable emotions, my mind spews a bunch of thoughts/reasons why it would be so nice to eat chocolate cake. I could be in the middle of my dilemma and all of a sudden the powerful allure of cake, chips or food in general, takes an immediate and firm grip on me. Other people may be attracted to things like excessive shopping, drugs or alcohol. The problem is not eating the cake, buying lots of stuff I really don't need, or getting high or drunk. Those are symptoms. The problem is that I wasn't processing my uncomfortable emotions, created by my prior thoughts. I was resisting them. This is the cause. Overindulgence is the symptom.

It's at this point of uncomfortable emotion, that the brain prompts us to go get some back-up. This is in an attempt to keep these unpleasant emotions at bay. The mind prompts us to get such back-up as food, a cigarette, or alcohol, to help push those uncomfortable feelings down or away. Let me point out that some behavior is not a major problem unless it is in excess and/or is being used as a means to an end that doesn't serve you. Excessive anything isn't the issue, it's a symptom.

Whether or not you handle your emotions well, get sidetracked with a feeling of uneasiness, or you believe you have an outright addiction to something, emotions that are not fully felt in the moment leave something of themselves behind. This creates what we refer to as baggage. Some of us have more baggage than others. Some of us process our emotions as they arise, accruing very little baggage. We should all be so lucky.

Excessive anything isn't the issue, it's a symptom.

Processing my emotions is another topic for which I can use the analogy of a small child. Did you ever see a small child that's upset? Their little faces register the discomfort of their emotions produced by their thoughts. As soon as the chance arises, they come running into the arms of a loved one. The child doesn't even speak. All they want is to be held. You embrace and comfort them. No words are necessary. This is all they want. This is all they need. Before long, as if by magic, they go running off happily in another direction. The magic lies in silently feeling the physiological feeling of the emotion, in the body itself. It is the momentary pause of silently feeling.

Emotions, like small hurting children, only want to be embraced and they will happily go running off. That's all the emotion wants. Feeling it, is what's healing it. Learning a practice of processing your emotions not only allows you to drop a load of unwanted baggage, whether you know you're lugging it around or not, but it also clears your path for growth, achievement and greater happiness. Yeah, that last part was big and exciting news to me too. (Of course, if you've experienced excessive trauma, I urge you to venture into acknowledging it with the help of a professional.) One of the most valuable books I've read on the subject of emotions is *The One Thing Holding You Back*, by Raphael Cushnir. The book includes Cushnir's pioneered method of emotional connection. It is a simple, effective and invaluable practice.

Feeling it, is what's healing it.

There is plenty of information out there on stress and its ill effects on the body. Of course stress doesn't just inexplicably appear, sneak up on you, and smack you in the back of the head. It's produced by our thoughts. By the same token, there is also plenty of information out there on the wonderful effects a stress-free life has on the body. Ah, feel-good thoughts don't only feel good, they are good for you. :) It sure pays to swim in the clear, happy waters of the outer ring of the pond. Of course it's even better to reach the shore which enables you to perpetuate that happy swim without ill effects. This brings me to what I feel is an important point. When we feel bad in some way, our knee-jerk reaction is to stop it, change it, fix it. I get that and I think that's a novel idea. But not so fast, we don't want to throw out the baby with the bath water. In other words, emotions and feelings, in addition to having a great hand in what kind of experiences we have, serve another purpose. They are messengers.

So my Higher Self is the Captain, the Pilot, and my thinking mind best serves as the first mate, or co-pilot. In doing so, how does the thinking mind take direction from the Captain? How does it receive the information as to where to turn left or right? How does it know when to choose yes or no, this thing or that one? The Higher Self can relay the reading of the inner compass through the body.

The Higher Self can relay the reading
of the inner compass through the body.

Sometimes sensations and feelings are subtle, sometimes they are prevalent and undeniable. Many people have told stories about how they were overwhelmed with a feeling of "Stop. Wrong way, do not proceed.", and it ended up possibly saving their lives. The body serves as a barometer or an alarm clock of sorts. There are times we are spontaneously prompted to do something that may not make logical sense to our thinking minds, but when followed, turn out to be very beneficial. These things are sometimes referred to as miracles. One of the things I know for sure is that the mind lies, the body does not.

One of the things I know for sure is
that the mind lies, the body does not.

How does one differentiate between thought-produced feeling and a feeling produced by higher Intelligence? This is sort of like learning how to walk. We take one baby step after the next. With each step and fall, we learn. We learn not to put our foot too far out ahead of us. We learn to get up. We learn to lean more this way or that. What we do not do is get discouraged and give up. We, as babies, just keep getting back up and trying it again until we walk. Babies do not give up on honing their skills. It would do us good to continue this practice of sticktoitiveness. Learning the difference between thought-produced feeling and a feeling produced by higher Intelligence is no different. Practice.

Should I take that job and move cross country? Feel. Turn down the volume in the head as much and as often as possible. Get Present. Come into this moment, right now, and feel. Feel for the yes or no, hot or cold, stop or go of it. You may even feel guided to do something completely different than your original plan. In silence, you can feel the aliveness of the body. In the aliveness of the body, you can feel your guidance.

> In silence, you can feel the aliveness
> of the body. In the aliveness of the
> body, you can feel your guidance.

What? You didn't get an immediate and clear answer? So what. Whining, worrying and believing your thoughts before questioning them, only render you unconscious and suck you into muddy water. I don't know about you, but I'm sick and tired of going that route. I'm full, no thanks. What I do now when I don't get a clear and quick answer is.....nothing. That's right, no splashing around and swimming in circles for me. I let it be, and wait. I ask, then I wait. I stay Conscious. Eventually and inevitably I recognize a prompting. I recognize a feeling of hot or cold, yes or no, good or bad, like or dislike.

Right here, I would be remiss if I didn't reiterate the importance of acceptance. If, for example, you really want to go on a date with that guy or gal and you are experiencing one "coincidence" after the other that prevents you from getting there, I'd recognize and heed the sign posts. The sign posts could manifest themselves in the form of locking your keys inside the car, or a sudden blast of diarrhea right before you leave the house for your date. Remember, your Higher Self is always on your side. It will always, no matter what, act in your highest good. If I allow my thinking mind to talk me out of knowing this, well.....I'm on my own. Getting quiet and becoming familiar with my own guidance is one of the best things I can ever "do."

Turn down the volume, and feel. :)

PART THREE

ACCEPTING, ALLOWING, ATTRACTING, OH MY

- 9 -

It's Not My Job Man

There are many of us that say we believe in a Higher Power. Although there are many words or names used to reference this omnipotent Source Energy, here I'll refer to it as God. If you ask people if they believe God is the omniscient, benevolent creator of all things, pure Love itself, they would probably say yes. So would I. So what's the story? Is God all of those things...except for this one little situation in my life, where I know better, because I'm sure things are not as they should be? Cue the Ah-Ha moment.

I can hear the swirling of thinking minds. "Do I have any control at all? Do I still try to focus on good thoughts? Do I take the bad things and try to see the good in them?" Our minds are at the ready, waiting to jump in and do something so that the events in our lives unfold the way the mind thinks they should. Our minds mean well, and they do not want to hear that it's not their job to manipulate how our lives should unfold.

Let's say your mind has a long list of all the reasons why it knows you should get the promotion you applied for. Maybe you even wrote them down. Great! Now you can throw it in the garbage. You can now stop thinking about it. You don't have to figure it out. You don't have to contemplate the how of it. Realize that if you think your control lies in your thinking, you're lying to yourself.

It's certainly nice to have a plan, or to revel in a feel-good daydream of your new corner office. Good, go for it. It's when you go unconscious and get lost in believing the story of the promotion that you're wasting your own time, so to speak. And even in that there is a lesson. The Universe gives us the best thing, person or situation we need, at the perfect moment we need it for our growth.

The Universe gives us the best thing,
person or situation we need, at the
perfect moment we need it for our growth.

The concept of allowing, and not allowing, does not translate to either attracting "good" things into my life, or attracting "bad" things into my life. The mind assigns the "good" or "bad" labels and then lists reasons to support those labels. Reasons are what we use to formulate beliefs. What the concept of allowing means is that I am either in acceptance or in resistance to what is, and moreover, all that is, is good. I don't have to pick or choose how events will unfold. Allowing (what is) is acceptance and not allowing (what is) is resistance. Either way, whatever is happening, or not happening, is good for me. Just because my mind can't or won't see it, doesn't change this Truth.

What the concept of allowing means is that
I am either in acceptance or in resistance
to what is, and moreover, all that is, is good.

When I am in resistance to what is, I will experience anything from mild discomfort to outright suffering. The good news is that you don't have to like something to get the gift out of it. Look at it. It's there. If my mind is churning out its conjecture anyway, then maybe instead of burning the midnight oil on all the reasons why something stinks, I can try burning that same oil on all the ways this thing may be in my favor. When I can, I stop. I let it go. I go back to practicing lowering that volume in my head. I let the Universe do what it does. It's really a lot easier than we tell ourselves it is. Allow and accept. Let it be easy.

When I had the realization that I could rip up and throw away my to-do lists, it made me very happy. I'm not saying that to-do lists are bad or they are not helpful. What I'm saying is that I realized I did not have to live my life by them. I don't have to live life like it was just a series of things to be accomplished. I can let go and accept, knowing that if I'm quiet I will be guided into inspired action, if any action at all, and everything will fall into place.

I can let go and accept, knowing that if I'm quiet I will be guided into inspired action, if any action at all, and everything will fall into place.

For me, letting go and accepting is the meaning of faith. When I realized that I did not have to always do, do, do, it felt like a load was taken off my shoulders. The shoulders that were usually up around my ears, unconsciously of course. It's funny how that works. You could walk around with your teeth clenched, your shoulders up around your ears, or with a look on your face like a low, steady stream of electricity is slowly electrocuting you, and not even be consciously aware of it!

In addition to carrying around beliefs that aren't true, I've learned that carrying around a load of unprocessed emotion has the same effect as a slow electrocution. Some of us are carrying around a lot stuff. Stuff that may feel too painful to process, stuff we may not even be consciously aware of. Lugging this load of unprocessed emotion and debilitating beliefs through life becomes cumbersome. It casts a shadowy impact on all facets of our lives. It just plain gets in the way of living life. It has a cumulative effect. I'm in resistance to a little of this, I'm not allowing a little of that.

The trouble is that when you add to your load of stuff little by little, it's harder to notice the collective increase. It's kind of like gaining a few more pounds than you expected over the holidays. I found myself wondering why things seemed so difficult, why I felt so exhausted and ineffective, and why nothing seemed to work out. If that wasn't bad enough, I've come to learn that I was the only one that didn't see the load I was carrying. : o

The bottom line is, if I'm experiencing a tough time, I may be harboring some unprocessed emotions. I may be believing some untrue thoughts, and/or I may be in resistance to what is.....which already is.....it's already like that, whether I like it or not. Fighting something that already is, is just wack-a-do behavior. Yes, we all exhibit that kind of behavior from time to time. If it already is, accept it and let it go. Okay, now you've just empowered yourself. :) I recognize my tough time as a sign post, a red flag, or an opportunity. If I can spare myself the effort of resistance, I am free to use that effort where it would be most beneficial.

The more I practice acceptance, the more the things I deem uncomfortable seem to just fall away. I don't have to do anything about it unless I'm motivated to do so, outside of the mental scrutiny of it. I try moving on to a moment of no thinking. That's always an empowering thing I can "do." I just may get a moment of magical guidance, motivation or inspiration in one form or another. Or, I could just bla, bla, bla it up in my own head until I feel like I want to poke myself in the pupils. So I have to take a few shots at it before I get the hang of it. So what. I accept that too. It's all for me. ;)

When I practice acceptance it opens doors, so to speak, that may not have opened at that particular moment otherwise. That particular moment is when I could really use an open door, or it wouldn't have shown up in the first place. Don't worry, the open door, or gift, will come around another way, another day, and knock again. Being in resistance is like pressing yourself up against the door, making sure your little miracle can't get in. Practicing acceptance allows my highest good to magically appear and find it's way to me. I accept, and sure enough, some "coincidence" that's in my favor occurs. I'm ready to do my part, and I don't get in the way. Allow, accept and voila!

Being in resistance is like pressing yourself up against the door, making sure your little miracle can't get in.

10

The Same Tomato

If you choose not to fight, you'll have peace. Or you can say, if you choose to see the "what is" of a situation, you'll have peace. Another translation would be, if you choose to allow peace, you'll have it. Accept and allow. Of course, if you have peace inside of you, you will see peace outside of you. This is another translation for "like attracts like." Accept, allow and attract. There's room for everyone at the Semantic Inn. ;P

We hold the belief that if we have control through our thoughts and choices, nothing "bad" would happen to us. We would have the power, the control, to stop that thing and have this thing instead. Sometimes it seems as if our experiences tell us that we do not have any control over our lives. Well, we do. We just don't realize that we really don't need it. So, we go to great lengths for control, as individuals and also as nations. If you believe you need control, know this is a fear-based thought. Red flag, red flag! Fear-based thoughts are lies.

I used to wonder why control seemed like a human priority, whether it was translated as a constant underlying whisper or came across as obvious as a fist-clenched fighting stance. Our collective desire for control shares a lowest common denominator, fear. We could speak endlessly about control, but we don't have to, because all of these roads lead to the same onion. Peel back all the layers of why we believe we need control, and on the inside we will find fear.

Our collective desire for control shares
a lowest common denominator, fear.

For example, say a small team of people are working on a project, and they want a project leader. I think I should volunteer to be the project leader. Why? "Because I want the project to be successful." Why? "Because if the project is not successful we may all look bad. The project may not be all that it could be. I may look inept if I don't step up. This may be the very project the next promotion is based on. Our project would benefit more people if I were able to execute my plan." These are the thoughts/reasons my mind offers to confirm it's belief that I should be the project leader.

Even if my intentions are considered well-meaning, they are fear-based. I have no way of knowing if any of my reasoning about being the project leader is actually true. When asking myself why I wanted to be the project leader, I said, "Because I want the project to be successful." Do I know for sure the project will not be successful if I'm not the project leader? No, I can't say I know that for sure. I also offered the reasoning, " Because if the project is not successful we may all look bad." Do I know for sure that we will all look bad if the project is not considered successful? No. Do I know for sure what other people will think of us, and do I have any control over what other's think? Uh, no. The need for me to want control is based on fear. I would be afraid others would not think as highly of me if the project was unsuccessful. I would be afraid of being considered inept. I would be afraid of being passed over for a promotion.

The only reason we believe these types of thoughts, is because we've briefly dozed off into unconsciousness. We wake up and free ourselves from these limiting beliefs when we remember that everything is as it should be. Everything is in the space it's supposed to be at the exact time it's supposed to be there. Nothing is a coincidence. We are loved and all is truly well, even if we can't see it from where we are standing.

There is nothing we have to do to secure our own happiness, outside of being *inspired* to do something. All we have to "do", is to allow. If I got passed up for a promotion it would be because that was in my highest good. When I allow myself to see the Truth in that, I open the door to my highest good, instead of closing it in fear. Any feel-bad thought is a fear based thought. They are one and the same.

There is nothing we have to do to secure
our own happiness, outside of being *inspired*
to do something. All we have to "do", is to allow.

What if it is in my highest good to be the project leader? How would I know if I should volunteer? I know I should volunteer, if I do. If I'm inspired to volunteer outside of the fear-based thoughts my mind creates. So how do I know if I am really inspired to be the project leader? Hmmm, project leader....how does that feel to me? Does it sound like fun? Does it make me feel excited? Does the thought of doing that make me feel happy?

There are people who say that at the core of their onion is happiness, and that happiness is the ultimate reason for wanting control. I can see that. So, do you believe that if you don't stay in control of things, you may have less of a chance of experiencing happiness? If you do, that's still a fear-based belief. Whether we want control because we believe we are trying to move away from something, or we want control because we believe we want to push toward something, it's all still fear-based. I get it, though. I'm using the same software. Stick with me, we're getting to the part where we can actually do something and not stink like a scared little onion.

Whether we want control because we believe we are trying to move away from something, or we want control because we believe we want to push toward something, it's all still fear based.

Instead of spending ten dollars on poison, spend the same ten dollars on a healthy meal. There's our control, in our choices. We can start by accepting what is. Even, and especially, when the what is stinks. Sometimes we can't see happy from where we're standing. Sometimes we feel like we are at the end of our rope. If I can't see beyond the horizon, that's okay. I Accept and allow. I am not condoning anything, I am only accepting that it is the way it is, in that moment. This actually frees and empowers me. If I feel the need to stop the chaos in my head, and I feel like I just can't turn it off, I swim toward the happy part of the pond. I use my mind to my favor and I think of things that will change my state to one that is more comfortable, even happy.

We are all capable of coming up with one little feel-good thought. Yet sometimes, coming up with a feel-good thought may feel like it's just too hard to do. The first step in getting beyond this situation is to accept it. Now, if I am still having a little trouble finding a feel-good thought, I ask myself a provoking question. "If I were able to have a happier thought right now, what would it be?" I listen, and sure enough something will pop into my mind. I don't judge or rate it. I gratefully accept it. I allow more good thoughts to come to me by keeping my Focus on the subject of good thoughts. Thinking good thoughts, brings more of the same.

One thought, any old thought that feels good invites another one, and another one. They don't have to create a story. They don't have to be related in any other way than that they just feel good. It's all about where I put my Focus. Focusing on good thoughts leads me to feeling relief, to feeling pretty good, to feeling pretty great. There's no harm in that. As a matter of fact, feeling good is an inside job. It is my responsibility. Eventually these types of choices will look a lot like the kind of control that makes my thinking mind feel secure, confident and safe. That feels good.

I allow myself the freedom to know that feeling good in this moment is what's most important, not unraveling a knot of feel-bad thoughts, even if I've labeled it an urgent "problem". Why? Well, the obvious reason is because feeling good feels good, but that's not all there is. Feeling bad is a sign post that we are headed away from our highest good. I don't want to make decisions when I'm facing in the wrong direction. I don't want to figure it out in my head, when my head can't see North.

I allow myself the freedom to know that feeling
good in this moment is what's most important,
not unraveling a knot of feel-bad thoughts,
even if I've labeled it an urgent "problem".

I untangle myself first. How do I know when I'm untangled? I know I'm untangled when I feel good. I choose *for* me. I don't forget to squeeze in a few moments, as often as possible, when I turn down, or turn off, the interior volume all together. Whenever I can, I stay Present in my own life. I should probably be more specific to say that by doing these very things, I've come closer to the shore, and to experiencing the peace and happiness that is the ultimate desire of all of our doing. All of our doing is pointing to the same place. We are all pointing to happy.

11

I'll Take One From Column A and Two From Column B

Sometimes our life experiences seem to be going well. We feel happy about that and we readily accept it. Sometimes our life experiences seem to not be going so well. We judge an experience as bad because we don't see our higher good in it. We resist, and then we feel unhappy. You don't have to like, or agree with, your circumstances to feel better about them. Remembering to notice the actual isness of a situation, and accepting that it already is, is the first step.

Choose what feels better. Does it feel better to think of how many ways this situation could turn into a train wreck? Or, does it feel better to think about how many ways this situation can work out well for you? Does it feel good to think about that castle you wanted for your tenth birthday? Then do it. Does if feel good to think about having admirers or suitors? Go for it. What? You want to know what thinking about being a drug to the opposite sex has to do with the "problem" at hand? To that I say, I believe feeling good is the ultimate feeling we are all after. Why not cut right to the chase? Choose *for* you. Let it be easy. Allow.

I'm not saying to allow that annoying guy from Accounting to continue to flick you in the eyebrow whenever he sees you. I'm saying, you would deal with that a lot better if you feel good, empowered, and in control of yourself, rather than if you feel a seething desire to drop kick him in his pocket protector. Okay, okay sometimes fantasizing about that spontaneous roundhouse kick could bring a happy little snicker to your face, so use that to swim over to the happy side. I'm assuming here that you have a tad of common sense. If not, don't use that technique. :/ This may be your chance to practice assertiveness, "Stop doing that." Accept whatever the what is is, then choose thoughts that work in your favor. Sometimes we have to swim from the dark, cold center of the pond, to the happy outer ring of the pond, to eventually get to the shore. Choose what will get you there.

If you were to walk from New York to Chicago you'd have to take a whole lot of steps to get there. If New York represented where you are now, and Chicago represented where you longed to be, make the choices you feel will get you there. Go with your own flow. When you make a choice, silently feel what that feels like. Does it feel good? Yes, it's that simple. Simple yes, but not always easy. Still, so totally doable. What? You can't decipher if it feels good or not? Try again. Still nothing? Try again.

When you make a choice,
silently feel what that feels like.

If you can't hear the doorbell from the basement, walk up the stairs and listen again. If you can't hear it from the stairs, go into the kitchen.....or the dining room. Eventually you'll hear it. It's not a question of whether or not there is anyone at the door ringing your bell. There is, it's you. Your inner Guidance. It's only a matter of whether or not you can hear it from where you are. You are never without what you need. Choose the baby steps that get you to your own front door. Alright, okay, I'm about to blow my own roof off with this metaphor. :/

My mind likes that little rush of excitement it feels when it thinks of the times that my best interest fell into my lap. I choose to remember all the "coincidences" that were in my favor. I choose to remind my mind that Serendipity isn't just a cool New Age name that works best with a one or two syllable surname. It's real. It sometimes translates as miracles. I choose to have some of those. I get going like the Little Train That Could when I think about how many choices I have that will empower me. That's much handier, and more importantly, it feels much better. I choose to make an effort to remind myself, as forgetting seems to be the thinking mind's narcolepsy. I post-it note my way into reawakening. I choose to remind myself to choose for me. It's a practice, a way of life. The ongoing isness of the human experience. Does it feel better? Does it feel good? I make an effort to feel my way in the right direction. I'm on my path to my highest good, where I occasionally go by the name, Serendipity Jones. : o

So do we have control or not? We have free will. We have choices as to where to place our Focus. We can choose things, thoughts and decisions, that make us feel better. So, yes, that is control. Can our thinking minds manifest what we want, when we want it? Outside of the occasional manifestation of some thing or situation we may have been focusing on, no, our thinking minds cannot do the Universe's job. At least not at this point in our evolution. The odds of our thinking minds consistently manifesting that specific person, situation or thing, at the perfect moment, for our highest good, is slim. Our thinking minds just don't have the capacity for that. The point is, we don't really need it. The Universe is already doing all of that for us. If I had the best of the best running my company, why on earth would I micromanage? Our thinking minds really don't know what our highest good is. The mind's choices are based on it's best guess of what may be in our highest interest. The good news is, the mind has the choice to check with inner Guidance. This way, the mind can at least determine if what it wants, is pointing in the same direction as the path to its best life.

The mind's choices are based on it's best guess of what may be in our highest interest. The good news is, the mind has the choice to check with inner Guidance.

Our minds produce a load of reasons that form the belief we need control. I don't have to believe it. This is a benevolent construct even though it sometimes seems otherwise. I realize I think I need to, should, and don't want to stop trying to control my experiences. But that's what my thinking tells me. My thinking lies. Do these thoughts produce resistance in me? If they do, it's only because somewhere in there I still believe I need to have control. And that's okay. Still, everything is as it should be. I believe I need to have control because I am afraid I will not be happy if things don't go as I plan. This is a common thought. However common this thought may be, it does not mean it's true. I remind myself to take the short cut. I remember that all I want is to feel happy. Feeling happy is always the most advantageous starting point.

I remind myself that the mind doesn't always care if I end up feeling happy, depressed or frustrated. It just wants to do what it does, think. For the purpose of this explanation, let's assume we are not aiming at keeping the whining at full throttle. If I can't immediately see through the untruths that my mind uses as a means to it's ends, I just choose thoughts that will make me feel happy. Sorry thinking mind, I know how you love a good parade, but I just want to get to the feel-good part. If I can't jump out of the pond onto the shore, I'll choose what feels good, what makes me happy, what gets me there.

> If I can't just jump out of the pond onto the shore, I'll choose what feels good, what makes me happy, what gets me there.

- 12 -

A Call to Action

I'm not implying you should just stay put like a bump on a log. If you feel a call to action, go for it. Apply for that job, jump out of the way of that oncoming bus, don't take candy from strangers. Okay, that last thing isn't actually an act of "doing" anything, and that applies too. Doing is not tabu, it's part of the equation.

Action that comes out of an unconscious dialog is the kind of action that, more often than not, takes you in the wrong direction. Why? Because when we are submersed in the stories rambling in our heads, and we believe them before we question them, there is a great chance our plan to action is fear-based. Any plan to action rooted in fear will result in discomfort and turbulence. The path to our highest good is the smooth, easy road where you glide the effortless and enjoyable ride. It's where things, people and situations seemingly fall into your lap at the perfect time. Think about it for a sec. I'm sure you can remember a time when you experienced a "coincidence" that worked out in your favor. You were on your path. So who the heck would want to take a side road?

When I exit the path of my highest good onto the off-ramp of unconsciousness, I wonder why things aren't working out for me, and why things seem so difficult. The reason is that I've only implemented half the equation. Action needs to be coupled with Consciousness. I can feel my own Guidance, inside the blissful silence of my body. Action that serves my highest good is Presence based, not fear based action. Action coupled with Presence is the only way to fly. It's the yin and yang of the human experience. It goes together like peanut butter and jelly, pen and ink, like dancing and Prince music.

Action that serves my highest good is
Presence based, not fear based action.

Over the years, I have filled notebooks with written exercises, lists, affirmations, and more. Within the sea of concepts and techniques, practicing the Law of Attraction seemed very intriguing. Many of us are practicing The Law of Attraction. We are making an effort to manifest some of our wants. We may be pretty good at making lists, visualizing or meditating as a means of manifestation. That's great, especially if we're having fun doing it. Eventually, I began questioning my wants. This led me to a greater understanding of wanting, to say the least.

Let's take a look at where our specific wants come from. Do you want to be a basketball star because you are attracted to the prestige and respect you believe you'd get? (BTW, I'm not implying that that's a bad thing. It may be illusionary, but it still serves its purpose.) Or, do you want to play basketball because when you do, time stops, and you feel more alive and elated than ever? There's a big difference.

We all have something that sets our gut aflame with joy. Something that totally engages us in a fulfilling way. This is true even if we haven't yet stumbled across it. Actually, when you do anything in Presence, you are able to experience it in a way that makes your heart sing. Now I finally understand why people get off so much on jumping out of planes and dangling from cliffs. They are Present in those moments.

Wouldn't it be a kick in the pants to be so busy working your butt off trying to be that great basketball star, that you never discover that painting portraits makes your soul sing? I have a sour puss on just thinking about that. The mind makes major decisions based upon what our, often hidden, core beliefs and desires are.

The mind makes major decisions based upon
what our, often hidden, core beliefs and desires are.

There are some desires that serve as guidance to the life of our dreams, and some that are illusionary, and veer us off of the road to the life of our dreams. What?! Yeah, don't panic. Remember, it's simple, not always easy. I will learn to see the difference between the two when I do things like question my thoughts, check in with my gut, process my emotions and practice acceptance. Or, when I'm Present. Hey, if you think about how much time and effort we spend trying to find our best life in unconsciousness, I don't think those couple of little practices are that back-breaking. Besides, the more we Awaken the easier it gets for us to see the Truth. Moreover, all desires, no matter what labels we slap on them, are sign posts. They are all good.

There are some desires that serve
as guidance to the life of our dreams,
and some that are illusionary and veer
us off the road to the life of our dreams.

Sign Posts tell us we are either traveling with or against the current, toward or away from our highest good. Desires that point us to our best life feel warm, happy and work out well. It's our best life trying to get to us. We don't always accept and allow things we like, because they don't always look like what we thought they would. Because of this we end up discarding the very things we enjoy, which are the things that lead us to our optimal lives. We end up taking a longer, bumpier road to the life of our dreams. Desires that don't point to our best life, usually fight or elude us. Either that or they do turn out the way we persisted, uh I mean expected, only to leave us unfulfilled. This would be characteristic of pursuing a mind-made desire that is not in our highest good. When we have a hard time of it, we are in resistance or we are unknowingly believing untruths. How could I free myself if I don't realize I am in bondage? I can't. Then I don't, and I suffer. Screw that.

In the meantime we're making decisions based on what we think we really want, "I want to be a basketball star." Inside, what we really desire is to feel respected and admired. The thinking mind determined being a great basketball player is the way to achieve that. If you think about it, there are also a number of other careers that would produce those feelings as well. The mind just took its best guess. "I really like playing basketball, so this must be it, my one and only true calling." The mind made the call without checking the built in guidance system. So there you go, off and running in a direction that may make your thinking mind kind of happy for awhile, if you work hard enough. If it doesn't work out the way your mind planned, you suffer. And all the while, we don't realize the real reasons we're doing it all. :/

These career and relationship choices made by the thinking mind, are representations of the things we really want, deeper inside ourselves. And when we are submersed in believing stories, we are unconscious. So what can I do? Do what you love. Hone in on what you like instead of only believing the unquestioned scrutiny of the mind. What you have an affinity for, what you love, will always take you in the right direction. How do you tell the difference? Practice. Be silent. Check in with your gut. Question your thoughts. It's always simple, not always easy, and it's totally doable.

In the meantime, we have our eyes shut tight in visualization, and we're pinning up our vision boards. We're making wish lists in an attempt to attract that which we believe we want into our lives. Hold on, no where did I say or mean to imply that any of that is "bad." My point is that we are doing, doing, doing. That's not a bad thing either, but if it's not inspired doing, it may veer you off your road and it's probably not necessary. Scratch that, it's definitely not necessary. There is a clear bottom line. There is unconscious doing and there is Awakened, Inspired doing. There is unconscious attraction and Conscious attraction.

There is unconscious doing and
there is Awakened, Inspired doing.

The car, the house, the promotion is not the thing we are really after to begin with. Even though we believe we are damn sure of it, right down to the make and model number. Cars, houses, and promotions are just the kind of things the thinking mind assigns to our core desires. Core desires for things like prestige, security and respect. There is nothing "wrong" with that. If you are not attached to having a thing, and you simply admire it, thinking you could have a lot of fun with it, then go for it. The point is, it's helpful to determine if your mind is really after something that you were unaware of. Ask yourself why you want something. When you get that answer, ask why again, and again. This line of questioning will peel back your onion. If you discover a core belief that is based on untruths, or resistance to what is, you now have a chance to free yourself from it. You are now free to feel your way toward desires that serve as guidance to your best life.

For example, if I'm dead set on getting that promotion and I discover a core belief that says I need to feel superior, then that's a core desire based on an untruth. I'm already whole, I'm not missing anything. I'm not inferior. I may think I feel the need to feel superior, but it's only because my mind doesn't see that as the illusion it is. The need to feel superior, or whatever it may be for you, is a fear-based belief built on a multitude of related thoughts. It does not mean it's true. Fear and need exist only in the unconscious mind. There is no fear in Consciousness. There is no need in Consciousness. Our true happiness and subsequent success resides in Consciousness.

Fear and need exist only in the unconscious mind.

The things in my life are the representations that my thinking mind assigns to my core beliefs. If we take a closer look at some of the things that are in our lives, we will find this extremely telling. If most of my stuff is subpar, maybe I need to take a look at how I really feel about myself. On the shinier side of this coin, we all have some things, people or situations in our lives that are great. Even so, I'm not going to limit my joy and happiness on only what my mind can conjure up. I'm grateful for all the mind's well meaning work, and still I remind it to check in with the Captain, my guidance, my Higher Self.

I'll take that happiness and fulfillment in whichever way the Universe wants to offer it to me. Even if my thinking mind doesn't think it's shinny enough, fancy enough, expensive enough or whatever enough. Why? Because I know that no matter what form it comes in, I will be elated. What the Universe brings me will be ideal. I can not be sure what the mind pursues will have the same outcome. That's like choosing to go to a library with 100 books instead of the library with a never ending supply of books. Why would I limit myself? Even my thinking mind has to admit that doesn't make good sense. I see this as a matter of the co-pilot trying to navigate without consulting the Captain. The Captain, the one who has the compass and road map to my own paradise. Am I going to settle for something that serves my ego more than it does my true and deepest happiness? Hell no.

Am I going to settle for something that serves my ego more than it does my true and deepest happiness? Hell no.

Mirror, Mirror on the wall, who's the best manifester of them all? What is the very thing, the element, the magical thing-a-ma-jig that actually manifests stuff? There's the million dollar question, pun intended. It goes back to what the Law of Attraction really is. What's in, is out. What? Okay, let's start with what it isn't. The Law of Attraction is not a metaphysical Santa Clause who, if you believe in hard enough, will slide a Lamborghini down your chimney. Although, my thinking mind really likes that story, I see The Law of Attraction as the mirror concept in action. Everyone and everything we experience here is a mirror aspect of what's going on inside ourselves. A manifested image of our thoughts, beliefs and emotions.

Let's say for example, I'm feeling empowered on the inside. I would be attracting into my experience whatever the Universe knows is the best form of empowerment for me, at exactly the right moment. Even if it is another thought of empowerment. Attraction, like attracts like. The outside will reflect the inside. The thing is, we seem to struggle trying to create our own experiences in our lives. It's hard to understand why the thing I am thinking about and visualizing isn't manifesting for me. Despite all of our doing, we can't always create or achieve what our minds believe we really want. Not on a consistent basis, anyway. This is sometimes hard to accept......there's that word again. And in resistance comes discomfort, but I digress. What manifests in our lives is not solely based on the mind focusing on the things it wants. What trumps this are the seeds of our core beliefs. This is what manifests in our lives, everyday, all day. Some of those desires serve our highest good, and some are bogus. Bogus desires are created out of believing untruths, and do not serve our highest good.

Whatever is going on inside of me is being reflected outward into everything I experience here in my world. Your insides are the source of your outsides. The Universe doesn't put as much emphasis on my new car as it does on my growth. God isn't as interested in my promotion as much as it is in my

Conscious expansion. What comes into my experience is what I need for growth in that moment, not so much what I think I need to satisfy my thinking mind, or impress the neighbors.

The Universe doesn't put as much emphasis
on my new car as it does on my growth.

This is not to say you can't have or enjoy a new car or summer home. Of course you can. However, I don't think the only reason I came here was to work toward getting things. I came for growth and the freedom of Conscious expansion. In my experience, that is what's most important and fulfilling. That said, the other thing I came to this place for is big fun, and that may include a few things. ;) I consistently find that the more I'm in acceptance to however the Universe wants to offer me growth, the better my experiences here get. In addition, I find the more my action is inspired action, as opposed to thought-based action, the easier my experiences get. I don't know about you, but I like it much better this way.

- 13 -

Accepting, Allowing, Attracting and Doing

Let's connect the dots. We are making lists, going on job interviews, increasing our workout sessions, taking classes, etc. In addition to all of these things, we can now utilize accepting, allowing and attracting in our doing. We may identify the new car we'd like to have, right down to imagining the feeling of the soft, comfortable seats. By asking ourselves why we want the new car, and peeling the new car onion down to the core, we discover that what we really want is the security we think a new car will bring (or whichever thing and core desire applies to you). Then, even though we can admire this specific car in an unattached way, we know the Universe is much better equipped at formulating the best thing, at the best time, out of the infinite possibilities there are, to fulfill our core desires.

So which comes first, the chicken or the list? Well, all roads lead to Rome, as the saying goes, but everyone wants to drive in the fast lane. If that's the case for you, I'd say start on the yellow brick road that begins with your onion core. What? Let's say your mind dressed up your onion like a Rocket Scientist with a PHD. When you peeled back the whys of why you wanted to be a Rocket Scientist with a PHD, you discovered the core desire was to feel important.

Start thinking about all the times in your life when you have felt important. Now that's the fast lane. Give yourself what it really wants, to feel important. Great! You are now free from the haphazard mind-made guesswork that veers you off track. If you are now feeling important, the thinking mind will move on to a different misunderstanding. :p In other words, if you discover your desire to become a Rocket Scientist was based on an untrue core desire, and you satisfy that desire, the desire to be a Rocket Scientist will fade. It will fade if it is not an authentic desire that comes from your Higher Self. You are now free to get back onto the path of your best life. With a little detective work you skipped right over 72 years of college and a lifetime of school loans. Not that there's anything wrong with education, I myself am a huge fan. And who knows, maybe your heart would really soar if you spent your life growing vegetables, or producing T.V. shows.

How can I find my way to doing something I love? Do the two-step dance. I ask myself what makes me feel happy. Then I take a step toward that. I don't get too hung up on what the thing is that I enjoy doing, as I know it's really about the dance. I repeat this two-step dance until I get good enough at it to glide through my life blissfully. The steps of this dance will lead you to what you love. Start with whatever comes to mind, even if it is just a short nap that will make you happy, and take it from there. If you are in acceptance, aware of your core desires and open to inspired action, you are on your way!

If you are in acceptance, aware of your core desires
and open to inspired action, you are on your way!

My body is my barometer and alarm clock. It feels. That's how my built in guidance system communicates with me. That's how I can tell if I am on the road to a life of my dreams, or if I have veered off into rough terrain. How do I feel, good or not so good? It's not difficult. It may just take some practice. With a little repetition I can knee-jerk myself into checking in to see how I am feeling. Many of us have had the experience of the hair on the back of our necks or arms standing on end. Or maybe the Guidance came in the form of goose bumps. However the feeling came, you may not have recognized it as your Guidance. "Wrong way sweetheart, turn back!" Or maybe the feeling was trying to say, "That's it, now you're getting warmer!"

We get warm, feel-good feelings when we partake in something leading us in advantageous directions. We like it. Then our minds tell us there are better things to do than whatever we are loving in the moment. Our to-do lists rear their ugly heads and collectively call our name like Jack Torrance, in The Shining, with his face peeking in through the splintered bathroom door. It's at that point we have to stop and ask, "Really Jack? Will the world end if I don't stop doing something I like, to go do something I really don't like? I think you're a liar Jack."

It's pretty much just a reconditioning. If you want to feel loved, think about times you've felt loved, or ways in which you could feel loved. I do not have to believe my mind if it tells me there is a person outside of myself that holds my happiness, or the love I want to feel. That's just not true. I am Love and the keeper of my own happiness. Overlooking this, the mind took it's best shot at guessing where it thinks I could find that feeling of love. Why hang on to or chase a relationship out of non-acceptance? That's a sign post. If I just allow it, the Universe will bring me the perfect thing in the perfect time to fulfill my authentic desires. The core desires that are part of my Guidance system, the ones that lead me to my optimal life. Not the kind of core desires that are illusionary or mind-made.

If we allow it, the crappy thing can be replaced with the fantabulous thing that our real dreams are made of. In other words, the thing that keeps not working out so well, will be replaced with something that works out perfectly. The good news is, physiological feelings do not depend on what is true. You could still feel good fantasizing about something that never happened in "real life." So go on ahead and make something up, you know, a daydream, a fantasy. Maybe instead of a wish list of specific stuff, you could make a list of the specific feelings that you're after. A wish list of desired feelings. Maybe a collage of images to the same end. You get it.

Good work! You are now on your way to realizing that you already have everything you need. What? The need to create, obtain, manifest, and even some desires, are illusions. What? Yea, if that blindsided you a bit, I'm sorry. The good news is, you do not have to get rid of your stuff just because you step into the realization that you already have everything you thought the stuff would bring you. But hey, until then, "Beep! beep!", enjoy the ride! There's nothing wrong with material abundance. :)

- 14 -

The Law of Attraction

Our minds take great sign posts, things that point us in the direction of Conscious expansion, and turn them slightly to point in other directions. We point them toward things we want, things we believe we desperately need. Our unconscious thinking interprets life in a way that serves the thinking mind instead of our Higher Selves and our best life.

The reason the thinking mind interprets is because it really doesn't know for sure what's in our highest interest. The mind takes its best guess at assigning its core beliefs to the objects, people and situations in our lives. By misinterpreting, or skewing the sign posts, I end up running in place and wondering where oh where is the life of my dreams.

The mind takes its best guess at assigning its core beliefs to the objects, people and situations in our lives.

Even if I could not see it from where I am right now, I know we are already whole and complete. I don't need anything I don't already have. When I do, I will have it. I am not saying to stop admiring that beautiful new home, in an unattached way. I could even pin up a picture of it and daydream about it, if that makes me feel good. I would be skewing my sign post when I believe I need it, that nothing else can bring me what this particular thing will and/or if I become attached to it. I would be detoured on the side road, believing the answer to my happiness lies in things outside of myself. Things that I could have, if only I got good at manifesting. There is nothing outside of me. I am everything I see. It all comes from me. It's all in the bigger picture. As my Consciousness expands, as I come to know the Truth, my big picture gets bigger and bigger. I am the picture.

Right now it feels like my mind is quietly sitting down cross-legged, and dropping its head into its lap, like a child does when it feels deprived and on the brink of a tantrum. It feels as if what I am saying is in an attempt to take away the mind's enjoyment of all of the things that go into manifesting. Most importantly, it feels as if I'm impeding the mind's efforts to get what it believes it needs or desperately wants. "You don't get it, I need that and I need to be in control of it all!" I get it.

When I'm Present, I can admire something without becoming attached to it. I could get enjoyment from it without believing I need it. I can come to know the freedom of each moment is greater than what my mind is telling me it needs. "Yeah, yeah so what?" Well, this translates to enjoying things at a far deeper level than we imagined. Acceptance and Presence will lead you to an enjoyment that's independent and fulfilling. It is not the kind of enjoyment that's susceptible to unconsciousness. That kind of enjoyment is fleeting and unfulfilling.

When I'm Present, I can admire something without becoming attached to it. I could get enjoyment from it without believing I need it. I can come to know the freedom of each moment is greater than what my mind is telling me it needs.
"Yeah, yeah so what?"

My mind thinks, "Yeah, great. Right now I just want to know how I can get the stuff I know will make me happy." If I get the house it won't satisfy that feeling of insecurity. Oh, I may think it does for awhile and as soon as I'm done hanging the curtains and over the novelty of it all, I'll be looking for security in something else. It never really was about the house. I'm never going to get any stuff anyway carrying around the belief that I need it, or that I want it so much. This kind of wanting implies that I am missing something.

If what you really believe under all of your manifesting efforts is that you are missing something - even when you don't realize it - then guess what happens? That's what you'll get more of. You'll experience situations that give you more of the experience of missing stuff. : o When we get more of the experience of missing stuff, we feel the want even more. And 'round and 'round we go on the unconscious merry-go-round. Either that, or we give up. "This crap doesn't work."

If I want that new home more than anything else, because I really want the security I think it will bring, then I must feel insecurity on some level somewhere inside of myself. It would serve me to recognize this. If I could identify my real desire, security, I could recognize it's contrast of insecurity inside myself. We have contrast in this place, this world of form. Remember, our core desires are also sign posts leading us in the direction of our highest good. My highest good lies in the realization that my feeling of insecurity is based on a bunch of thoughts packed up into a belief that is a lie. My highest good is in realizing the lie. We confuse this with believing our highest good is the stuff we so deeply desire.

My highest good is in realizing the lie. We confuse this with believing our highest good is the stuff we so deeply desire.

We don't actually need to get something as much as we need to get rid of something. The mind is using it's logic and is subject to the Law of Attraction at the same time. The Law of Attraction just is, and it just does what it does. It does it everyday, nonstop. Like attracts like no matter what the like is. Truth attracts Truth. Lies attract lies. The mind is just riding the Law of Attraction in the wrong direction.

> Like attracts like no matter what the like is.
> Truth attracts Truth. Lies attract lies.

If we came to know that we are already the ideal that we seek, then the Law of Attraction would be manifesting the mirror aspect of that. However, wanting something because you believe your happiness depends on it, leads to an unsatisfied need for more and more. None of which will ever satisfy the unconscious mind.

There was a time when I felt insecure by not having what I thought of as a reliable car. Fast Forward. I now see through that thought to the Truth, and realize the feeling of insecurity is an illusion. In a nutshell, how do I know that I didn't need a more reliable car at that time? I didn't have it. I now feel the feeling of security in knowing that the Universe is all good. God is love. God holds me in the palm of it's hand. Yes, these are just more thoughts that can formulate new beliefs. But these thoughts would formulate new beliefs of knowing and feeling that I am secure and abundant. That's much different than feeling insecure. Feeling abundant feels a whole lot better than feeling scarcity or insecurity. And, if I feel abundant and secure on the inside, I will begin attracting what abundance and security looks like on the outside. ;)

I'm not saying that the only goal is to rewire the brain. There's no freedom in exchanging old, rusty shackles for new shinny ones. I'm just pointing out why the Law of Attraction works the way it does for us. As we Awaken, our untrue thoughts just magically fall away and we come into the freedom and happiness that we Are. In the meantime, we can still change our minds, change our beliefs, and affect our experiences for the better.

There's no freedom in exchanging old,
rusty shackles for new shinny ones.

This brings us to the good stuff. Could you imagine what our beliefs would be when our untrue thoughts fall away?! I Am. I am whole and complete. In that I am a never ending, abundant supply of divine Isness. When we come to know this Truth, we will feel it inside of ourselves. When I hold this Truth and feel it inside of myself, it will be mirrored on the outside of me. Freeing myself from limiting beliefs, and coming closer to the Truth, will feel better and better.

There are contrasts and repercussions in this world of form. Yin and yang, up and down, cause and effect. The mind will recognize the effect of seeing more and more of the Truth as a beautiful, happy and abundant life. Oh, and we wouldn't have to do, do, do anything to get that. All we have to do is to allow our own Conscious expansion. Our Conscious expansion happens one realization at a time.

Our Conscious expansion happens one realization at a time.

So, in the meantime, until we begin to see the picture a little more clearly, we are all doing the best we can. It's in my best interest to identify the real crux of my desire, so that I can identify what it is I'm believing. The lie, or the Truth I see is what's inside of me. What's in is out. What I feel and believe on the inside of me, I see on the outside of me. *This* is the Law of Attraction. It works best with it's magical partners Accept, Allow and Inspired Doing. A magic formula.

What I feel and believe on the inside
of me, I see on the outside of me.
This is the Law of Attraction.

Baby steps are fine. They're perfect. ;)

PART FOUR

THE ROAD TRIP

- 15 -
Getting To The Shore

We've taken a glimpse at the bigger picture. I've shared my notes about who and where I am and what I have to work with. All of these things add up to having this human experience, and what kind of experience that could be. Now it's time to walk the talk. It's time to take all of this on the road and incorporate it into our lives. What I need to remember is always simple, although not always easy. I don't ever have to push myself too hard at anything, and if I do, I will remember that means I'm doing it "wrong". Pushing myself too hard would be forcing myself at the promptings of my thinking mind instead of being inspired by my inner Guidance. I'm aware falling unconscious will come and go and I accept that. I accept what is, and I observe my thoughts. I watch my mind and question the thoughts that don't feel good. I do all of this, or I don't, and whenever I do it, it is always at the right time. Everything is as it should be.

The Universe is generous and abundant. If there is any work at all to be done on my part, it will be inspired work that feels like play, and just looks like work. It's all about where I put my Focus. I have free will as to where to put my Attention. I place my Attention, or my present moment Awareness, on questioning my thoughts and accepting the what is of any situation. Waking up out of the stories of my thinking mind is freedom. I choose putting my Attention on these very things that enable me to experience this place in ways that surpass my wildest dreams.

I stay Present. As often as possible, I focus on the present moment and bring my Awareness to it, in silence. (We spoke about being Present back in part one, chapter 3, Presence.) I practice not-doing. I practice silence in my head and emotional connection in my body. I practice unconditional acceptance, and questioning my thoughts. I find touching base with my own Guidance, keeps me in my lane and in the game. I remind myself to stay Awake, even if that comes in the form of leaving little notes for myself. Little by little, making these practices a way of life becomes easier, and you find that you are awake and aware outside of the submersion of the thinking mind for longer periods of time. Life becomes more enjoyable. You feel happy and have no specific reason why. You realize you never needed a reason why. All of a sudden you realize you're seeing everything differently. Your understanding is expanded. You see a much bigger picture and the picture is clear and simple.

I find touching base with my own Guidance,
keeps me in my lane and in the game.

We have tools, tips, sign posts, techniques, the thinking mind and our own built-in GPS to help us realize there is a shore, and how to get to it. I'm referring to the shore of Consciousness, outside of the pond of unconsciousness that I spoke about back in part two. We can draw on any one of our tools, at any time, and immediately swim back over to the clear, happy waters. How do I access my tools? I put my Focus on making an effort to accept the isness of a situation. I put my Focus on questioning my thoughts. (We spoke about questioning our thoughts back in part one, chapter 4, Beliefs.) Or, I could focus on the many self-help techniques I've learned, in the many books available out there, that helped me to feel empowered. I use my Focus to access my tools.

On our way to the Awakened shore, we sometimes seem to run into what we consider to be "problems." We basically have two options that equate to either navigating around the problem or going through the problem. One option is seeing through our untrue thoughts to the truth. This is where you question your thoughts. The "problem" in this scenario, will fall away. The only work required is in making the inquiry. Here's where The Work of Byron Katie is invaluable, utilizing her four questions and the turn-around. (Remember, you can access The Work on Byron Katie's website.) If you question with an honest, open mind you usually get better results. Occasionally, the results culminate in a grand Ah-Ha moment and a rush of freedom, sometimes accompanied by angels singing. Well, it could. Of course it's possible to question your way through it on your own and have the same experience, singing and all. Seeing through a "problem" consists of acceptance of what is, and inquiry into that - including the truth about your part in it. If it makes you feel better, you can do all of this in the dim, quiet back room of your mind where no one else has any idea what's going on. Amazing, huh? You could find the keys to your own freedom and no one would be the wiser! Of course the elation may give it away.

Seeing through a "problem" consists
of the acceptance of what is, and
inquiry into that - including your part in it.

The other way to navigate a "problem" is to partake in one or more of the many other techniques out there that help get you from one side of the pond to the other. These techniques could be anything from tips on how to be more organized, to maintaining a positive attitude, to actual meditative techniques to calm and balance us.

Back in the day, in public book stores, I could find little more than books by Shirley MacLaine and Dr. Wayne W. Dyer, in terms of spiritual knowledge. Reading those books felt like drinking a tall, cool glass of water after being lost in the dessert for a week. Nowadays, there are ample books, CDs, DVDs, MP3s, etc., by a multitude of authors and teachers, classified into one of several dedicated sections. There are concepts, practices, instructions on written exercises, all helping you to find your own empowerment. It's the way we can effectively deal with "problems" and improve our situations when we don't realize we've dozed off.

We are not exactly popping Awake into Presence, so I am very grateful for all the people speaking about and pointing us directly toward the shore, toward Awakening. I am also very grateful for all the people that are teaching us ways and techniques to make our lives easier and happier. These ways may not specifically speak of and point directly to Awakening, but I believe some of these teachings were the very life lines I used, not only to realize there was a shore, but to eventually get to it, even sporadically.

We are all in the pond, unconsciously, at one time or another. Of course when you are Awake and Consciously taking a dip in the pond, all is well. I'm referring to the times during which we lapse into unconsciousness and are splashing around wondering how we got into this mess. We wonder why things like this keep happening to us. We contemplate who did and said what, and what we're going to do about it, as soon as we get close enough to that bastard to poke him in the eye.

My least favorite, are the times I felt stagnated. I tried desperately to unstick myself and change my situation to seemingly no avail. No matter how much time and effort I put into coming up with another idea about how to change my frozen life, nothing seemed to work. It's too bad I didn't notice earlier, that the glue on my feet was a sign post. It would have been so freeing to recognize that I was so ardently swimming upstream.

Sometimes we just don't see the isness of a situation. We try our best to figure it out instead of feel it out. Had it dawned on me that there was a possibility I was to change directions in life, I would have at least stopped all that running in place. I would have worked on dropping the old, and feeling out the new direction. I would have been able to recognize my "stagnated" situation as a time of metamorphosis, rather than a time of being so stuck.

We try our best to figure it out, instead feel it out.

We occasionally have trying times where we see our own pain and suffering more clearly than anything else. We are sometimes attached to our pain and suffering. That's okay, you don't have to see or let go of anything. You can keep the story and the plans. While you keep them, know that there are options, should you decide the load you're carrying is getting in the way of living your life. You can see the actual "what is" of a situation and the real truth in that, or you can use some of the other techniques out there that will get you from the inner feel-bad circle of the pond to the outer feel-good circle of the pond. The way you choose to get to the happy swim is really irrelevant. The important thing is that you remember you belong there. Simply put, remind yourself to stay Present, practice unconditional acceptance and question your thoughts.

So what's the difference between the two options? With the first option, you step out of the story of the thinking mind, drop the whole load, and get out onto the Awakened shore. What does that mean exactly? You become Conscious and realize there is no problem. The rest pretty much takes care of itself at that point.

With the second option you remain in the pond and the mind deduces what may be a solution to your "problem." Solution or no solution you are able to change your emotional state. You have the ability to go from sad to happy. Your power is your Focus. Wield your power for your good and feel better, no matter what. You can also use the mind to put your Focus on acceptance and questioning your thoughts and beliefs. If you choose to take this route, you may arrive at seeing your situation in a whole new light. You could have a realization, an inner shift, or an outright epiphany. It is a series of inner shifts, or realizations, that is the portal to Awakening.

It is a series of inner shifts, or
realizations, that is the portal to Awakening.

Focusing on feeling good is fabulous. By all means, get there if you can, whenever you can. Wanting to feel good is something we all have in common. We all, all of us in a body, have that same want, that same need. The farmer in the rice paddy, the little boy riding in the back of his mom's car on the way to his soccer game, and the high level executive on his way into a board meeting. We all want to feel good. In this, there is an innate, inherent longing we all know. A commonality we cannot deny. An essence of humanity that unites. That's because happiness is part of that which we really Are. We are indeed all beautiful little pieces of the One. :)

Once we realize our own greatness is indeed part of the One, we can partake in that right now, right here, by coming into the present moment and moving into living an Awakened life. Is it simple? Yes. Is it always easy? No, and sometimes it is easy. Is it worth it? Let me put it this way, there is nothing else. You are either Conscious, or you are unconscious. You either gain lucidity in this dream, or you don't. Don't get me wrong, you can still have a wonderful life without what we call Enlightenment. We are all on this journey. The gift of the journey is growth. There is no Truth that growth always has to be painful. Yet growth is sometimes painful, but that does not mean that it is not possible to grow in pleasure.

The gift of the journey is growth.

I believe there are some people out there that naturally do the very things I've been reiterating, like accepting what is, questioning their thoughts, and being Present in their lives. They do these things in an easy and unassuming way. They do it in such a natural way that they themselves don't even notice it. I've noticed that these people follow a road where helpful coincidences seem to fall into their path, and their lives always float toward their highest good. They exude balance, calm and happiness.

I've learned that if something works, don't even take the time to let the thinking mind try to label it. Just live it. The good news is that we have the ability to live this kind of a life right now. And there's more good news. If we can't jump out onto the shore, or if today we are not even aware a shore exists, we still have the ability to swim over to the happy place. We still have choices that create happy lives. Everything really is *for* us, including and especially our own Greatness. Wield your power for good. ;)

Wield your power for good. ;)

- 16 -

Sign Posts

Sign Posts come in many forms. They are things, people and situations that point us in the direction of our highest good. They point us toward our life purpose, the life of our dreams, and spiritual growth. These sign posts are always around. We don't always see them. Some of them wait quietly to be noticed, while others sound their alarms.

I have a name for the people that come into my life as sign posts. I call them Pointers. The truth is anyone can be a sign post or a Pointer. We do it without even being aware of it. We do it for each other. It's just part of the unfathomable synchronicity of this construct. I'm so very grateful to Pointers who do it on purpose, people like Eckhart Tolle, Byron Katie, Martha Beck, Dr. Wayne W. Dyer, Louise Hay, Shakti Gawain, Raphael Cushnir and the many others. Their pointing has helped to point so many people in the direction of their highest good.

Pointing is the most we could do for one another. Remember the sandwich? I can make you a sandwich, but you are the only one who could eat and digest it. I am the only one who can experience the realizations or Conscious expansion that lead to my Awakening. I'm grateful for the people who were my sign posts, the ones that kept pointing me toward things like being in the present moment, practicing acceptance, questioning my thoughts and processing my emotions.

I can make you a sandwich, but you are
the only one who could eat and digest it.

"Problems" are sign posts as well. I use quotation marks because problems don't really exist, at least not in the way we think of them. I know, I know, I could have fooled you. I have fooled myself plenty of times. If I believe everything happens for a reason, and that there is always a gift or a lesson in a situation, then how can I believe "problems" are bad things that must be avoided at all costs? I can no longer see it that way. Of course I still have a knee-jerk reaction to bracing myself in resistance to any potential "problem", and then I get real. I wake up.

I see that my "problem" is either pointing me in a different direction, or it's pointing me toward a realization. "Problems" serve a purpose, a purpose that is somehow in my highest good. More often than not, I just look past all the minutia and straight into that bag of poop for my pearl. If, for example, someone does something to me that certainly looks like it is not in my best interest, I remember it really has nothing to do with them. It looks like it does, but they are really only like messengers, relaying an opportunity. I also know what "problems" are not. "Problems" are not arbitrary, bad luck or coincidental.

I see that my "problem" is either
pointing me in a different direction,
or it's pointing me toward a realization.

The same holds true for "failures." There really is no such thing. The only way I can have trouble seeing how "failure" is a good thing, is if I'm believing my own lies, or am in resistance to what already is. Those would be two ways that I could overlook the empowerment waiting for me in the "failure." I would pass it up. That doesn't mean I loose my chance. That opportunity or lesson will just come around in another way, another day. If I don't get it then, it will just continue to show up in my life. I see this as the recipe for patterns. "Why is this happening to me again?!" The Universe will just keep offering me gifts, no matter how many times I turn them away, even unconsciously. Thank goodness the Universe never takes things personally! Had I not "failed" at finding the "job of my dreams" (AKA my thinking mind's guess at my best life), I would have never been led back to school, to learn new skills that I never thought I'd have. Skills that just happened to make themselves very useful, and helped to take me in a new and wonderful direction.

"Failures", like "problems", are sign posts. This could translate to "failures" and "problems" are opportunities. On the surface, it's difficult to see the Truth in that. These two words carry negative connotations, only because the thinking mind can't see them for what they really are. They are lessons, gifts, pointing us in the direction of our best life. In the past, I didn't realize that no matter what the Universe points at for me, it's in my highest good, even if my thinking mind had other plans. Boy oh Boy, my thinking mind sure had plans for everything. I now understand what a "problem" or a "failure" really is, and I can't help but feel gratitude. I process my emotions about them, and then I look for my pearls.

If I follow my sign posts, they will lead me to a greater fulfillment than my thinking ever could. And isn't that what we are all looking for? Isn't fulfillment the end all, be all, of why we try to navigate this human experience in the first place? We want to live a life that makes our Soul sing. We want fulfillment, fun, happiness and peace. We mistakenly think things like cars, homes, money, or fame are the source of our happiness. We mean well. We try hard. We don't have to.

Inside of every thing we want, is the real thing we are after. Someone that's driven to get that promotion into management may only really want to feel respected. Reach inside your dreams and find what your heart is really after. Then, recognize that you are surrounded by people, "problems", "failures" and ideas that are all pointing you in the direction of your best life.

Reach inside your dreams and
find what your heart is really after.

- 17 -
Waking Up To The Bigger Picture

So this is the bigger picture. We are not our thinking mind, nor are we the identity it created. We are Consciousness. And as for this place, well, it's a construct. It is an autonomous, benevolent construct. It's sort of like a dream. We did not come to Awaken from this dream, that would be what we refer to as death. When we are done with these bodies, these vehicles, and we "die", we are Awakening from this dream and going home. I believe death is like waking up in the morning and saying, "Wow, that was a good one! What a great dream! I learned so much. It was so much fun!" This is what I'm planning on saying when I get home.

We did not come only to Awaken from this dream, we came with the ability to Awaken *in* this dream. We came to exchange our fear-ridden unconsciousness and susceptibilities to pain and suffering, for Consciousness. We arrived with the ability to make this exchange. If we get a glimpse of the Paradise just over the wall, we can whisper into our neighbor's ear that he's been asleep, and for him to wake up, so that he doesn't miss all the great stuff. We have what it takes to create our best life and to create a new world. We have the ability to create our own heaven on earth.

We did not come only to Awaken from this dream, we came with the ability to Awaken *in* this dream.

It is what it is. It doesn't matter if we have a name or a mathematical equation for it, or not. The Conscious Universe already is, whether or not our frontal lobe can reason itself into thinking it understands it, or it doesn't. So why would I, the Consciousness that I Am, come to this place and into this body? There are so many stories the mind can conjure up in response to this question. The problem is, I'm aware of that, and I don't want any of those answers. I want the answer that comes from my gut. The answer that comes from outside of the words in my head. I want the knowing of it, not the minds

120

logical, analytical description of it. I believe one of the reasons we came here was simply to have fun. Maybe that's because we are the happiness we seek, and that's more literal than it is a cliche.

We can find the freeing, wonderful experience that exists in every moment. The experience of elation and awe that hovers in, out and around our very vehicle of form, and yet eludes us. Our experiences are squeezed and filtered through our thinking minds. We use this processed information to formulate our best guesses as to where our happiness lies. In doing this, we miss heaven right under our noses. Instead of feeding the stream of unconscious thought, I focus my Awareness on the spaces in between, the gaps, the invisible fabric of the Universe. I focus on the silence. It's in this empty space, that I feel a feeling of completeness, wholeness and that all is truly well. You will feel the knowing that sweating the small stuff is a painful misunderstanding.

You will feel the knowing that sweating
the small stuff is a painful misunderstanding.

I do believe in addition to coming here to have fun, that we also came to bring Consciousness into this world. But why? Consciousness is the very stuff this place is made of. Bringing our Consciousness into this world would be the exchange we make for the elation we could experience while we are here. Kind of like bringing some of your own sand into the sandbox so that we can have a nice place to play. BYOS, bring your own sand. Consciousness, is the raw material that this construct is made of and uses to perpetuate itself. Okay, so what if it is? My next question (because I always have one :/) is why?

Why would this place we call life want to perpetuate itself? That would take us full circle - so we could have some fun. Not just to have some fun, but to experience that which we Are, and bask in a bliss that goes beyond our best attempt at an explanation. That could easily translate to creating heaven on earth. We all have the ability to contribute. How I bring sand into the sandbox may be different from the way you do it. This does not require taking on a new endeavor or project. It is not a burden or a goal. You are not required to have a master's degree or to be some kind of guru. It can not be done with the thinking mind alone. It's not something you have to figure out. It's simply a byproduct of living an Awakened life.

When you do whatever it is you do while you are Present, you are bringing Consciousness into the world. This can easily be translated to creating a nice place to play, creating heaven on earth, or saving the world. Not to mention, living your best, happiest and most fulfilling life. Now that's a win-win situation. I didn't expect it would be any other way. And whatever way it is, it is. It's not necessary to understand it and it's not even necessary to talk about it. We already have everything we need. Everything that happens, happens for us, in the exact time we need it. This means that if I don't have the answer to the purpose of the Universe, or even the purpose of coming here to this place and being in this body, then I don't need it. We already have all the answers we need, when we need them. When we don't have them, we don't need them. Our minds feel the need to know, who, what, when, where, why and then some. We need only know Consciousness. Ironically Consciousness is the one thing the mind can not and does not know.

We already have all the answers we need
when we need them. When we
don't have them, we don't need them.

- 18 -
Shift Happens

I think I've sufficiently shaken this blanket out. I don't think there are anymore crumbs, not today anyway. I can throw this blanket down and I can relax. I can feel that freeing feeling of dropping an arm-load of baggage. I feel the peace, and the grin forming on my lips in the realization that I am the keeper of my own freedom. It begins with acceptance of what is, and being able to see through my mind's misunderstandings of the truth. These are the keys to our illusionary prisons. Once you have them and free yourself, you understand there was never really a prison to begin with.

I am the Gatekeeper. The Gatekeeper of my own happiness. Responsibility and choices are mine. I am the one who allows or does not allow. If some form of discomfort creeps in, I know it's because I believed the lie at the gate, and let it in. If I feel longing it's because I didn't recognize my higher good at the gate, and did not let it in. I now realize that self-love is the gate itself. I remember when my gate was weak and almost nonexistent. As a result I was unable to keep out the misunderstandings that were the catalysts of my pain and suffering. In Presence, comes Truth. In the Now, comes healing. In Consciousness, there is clarity. In Being, comes the shift.

In Presence, comes Truth. In the
Now, comes healing. In Consciousness,
there is clarity. In Being, comes the shift.

I do my best not to think my way through life as much as I feel my way through. I know the nucleus of my life experiences come from that small space inside of myself. If I don't make that small space work, I'll never get anything else to work. If I'm not happy on the inside I won't see happy on the outside. I know that there really isn't anything I need to do, if I am not inspired or guided to do so. That was big news for me. I was so conditioned to doing, doing, doing on unquestioned thought alone. I heard someone say the meaning of insanity is doing the same thing over and over again and expecting to get a different result. So, I (my thinking mind) tried every which way it could, to muster up new ways to try. Then, I realized.

I stopped splashing around. I let things be easy. I work hard, yes, but when I'm inspired to do so, not because my mind rapid-fires reasons that formulate untrue, fear-based beliefs. I'm not suggesting to go out on strike in protest of your own life. I'm suggesting to identify and follow the scent of feel-good all the way to your own promised land. Getting the hang of doing this may take a little time.

I'm suggesting to identify and follow the scent of feel-good all the way to your own promised land.

I'm not offering my notes on this human experience as the only rays that lead to the sun. There are many. You can find others. You can find your own. We can help point each other there. But we are the only ones who can get ourselves there. Find your way. If any one of us have experienced empowering revelations, that lead to freeing clarity and fulfilling happiness, that means we can all have that same experience.

We all want a happy life and a better world. The most we can do as an individual, is clean up our own backyard. This is the most any one person can do. We are the only ones who could do that for ourselves. There is no magic pill and there's no one you can hire to do it for you. The good news is that when we each clean our own backyard, the automatic result is a better world. It's a byproduct. That is the only way to create a better world, one clean, happy backyard at a time. One empowering and freeing shift at a time. When we have peace in ourselves we will see peace in the world.

The good news is that when we each clean our
own backyard, the automatic result is a better world.

Our happiness is an inside job and it's totally doable. It's so much easier than we think. We are, all of us, capable of Awakening and always seeing the good news. By the same token, by always recognizing the good news, we can Awaken. We don't have to be a spiritual teacher or guru. We don't have to be part of the clergy, a monk or a saint. Awakening is not reserved only for those who dedicate eight hours a day to deep meditation. It's for nurses, farmers, writers, parents, the unemployed, the sick, and the healthy. In it we find the realization that we have possessed the ability and choices all along. It is prefaced with the Ah-Ha moment of distinguishing between Consciousness and unconsciousness. We all have the ability to wake up *from* the dream. The life of our dreams lies in Awakening *in* the dream. Let's go.

Feel what makes you happy, what you like, and keep going back for more. Try floating happily with the current instead of swimming hard and fast against it. Don't sweat the small stuff. Nothing is that serious. Loosen up and have some fun. If you don't want to dive right in, just try walking some of this talk one day out of each week. When you create happy little pieces of your puzzle without having to control the bigger picture, the bigger picture comes to you.

When you create happy little pieces of your puzzle without having to control the bigger picture, the bigger picture comes to you.

Let go of always trying to put it all together. Focus on your little pieces of happy, of Presence, even if and especially when it may seem scattered and unrelated. One day, you will look up and see a picture even more beautiful than you imagined. A beautiful mosaic of all your little pieces. The life of your dreams, exactly as it is, exactly as it should be.

Now let's go have some fun. ;)

PART FIVE

MNEMONICS

Tips and Tricks to Kick Yourself Back Into Play

The good news is there is always good news.
We may not always see it, but our highest good is always there.

What a tangled web we weave, when first we practice to believe.
Question your thoughts.

When things go bad, be glad.
That's a sign post. You are either being pointed in another direction or being made aware of an opportunity for growth.

Feeling it, is what's healing it.

Embrace your emotions like you would a small hurting child. You will heal and run off happily.

When in doubt, don't.

Stop. Take some time, even a moment, to feel it out.

Don't scrutinize, recognize.

There was a flood. The waters were rising fast. A man's neighbors offered him a ride out of town. He said no, that he had faith God will save him. The waters rose higher and the man went up to the second floor of his home. A boat came by and the people told the man to jump in. He said no, that he had faith God will save him. The waters rose even higher and the man climbed onto his roof. A helicopter came by and the people told the man to grab onto the rope so they could get him to safety. The man said no, that he had faith God will save him. The man died. He went to heaven and told God how he believed God would save him from the flood. He wanted to know how this could have happened. God said, "Are you kidding? I sent you a car, a boat and a helicopter!"

It's always simple, it's not always easy.

We are either Conscious, or we are unconscious.

Stay in your lane, stay in the game.
Check in often with your own guidance to stay on the path of your highest good.

Quit splashing!
Float you're way to shore. Accept unconditionally.

B.Y.O.S.
Bring your own sand (into the sandbox.) Find the way in which you bring Consciousness into this world.

Your insides are the source of your outsides.
What you feel and believe on the inside is reflected in the world outside of you.

Intention is the mother of invention.
Intend the best. Let it come to you.

Focus is my magic wand.
I wield my powers for good.

Another way, another day.
If I can't see the Truth today, I know it is always there patiently waiting for me.

It's never too late to change my state.

At any moment, I have the power to think happy thoughts, or to get Present.

Resist Persisting.

Practice acceptance.

Stop, drop and question.

Question your thoughts, especially when you feel "negative" emotion. "Is this absolutely true?"

I am the Gatekeeper.

I am the keeper of my own happiness. It's all on me.

Do the two-step dance.

Step one: ask what would make you feel happy.

Step two: take a step toward that.

Repeat until you're dancing.

Don't figure it out, feel it out.

Come into the present moment and silently focus on your feelings about a subject. Good = go. Bad = no.

Let's go to the movies.
Be the unbiased Observer.

Help! I'm on the Crazy Train. :/
Getting Present is the equivalent of pulling the emergency brake.

Inside every hot bag of poop is a pearl.
Within every "problem" lies something of value.

When I don't feel as good as I did before, there must be a messenger at my door.
Uncomfortable feelings and emotions are messengers/sign posts that tell me I am believing an untruth, or I am in resistance to what is.

Like attracts like.
Truth attracts truth. Lies attract lies.

Don't just do something, sit there!
Practice not-doing.

Pass it forward.

This is the story of the Bodhisattva. The meaning of a Bodhisattva can best be understood in the story.

Three men were walking in the desert. They were thirsty, hungry and weak when they came upon a huge wall. They circled the wall, but could find no way in. The first man climbed onto the back of one of the other two men and started the long, arduous climb up the wall. When he reached the top, he look over and exclaimed, "Eureka!" He jumped over the wall and was gone.

The second man climbed onto the back of the third man and started the long, arduous climb up the wall. When he reached the top, he look over and exclaimed, "Eureka!" He too jumped over the wall and was gone.

The third man did not have the privilege of climbing on another's back and so he began his long, arduous climb up the wall. When he reached the top, he looked over and saw the most beautiful and plentiful valley, with cool, clear waterfalls, ample fruit trees and lush foliage. He, however, did not leap over the wall into this paradise. Instead, he made the long climb back down the wall and headed back out into the hot desert.

He went to search for other wanderers so that he may tell them about this paradise, and how to get there.

And he, is the Bodhisattva.

If we get a glimpse of the Paradise just over the wall, we can whisper into our neighbor's ear that he's been asleep, and for him to wake up, so that he doesn't miss all the great stuff.

-Gina

Glossary

: o	Surprise, wow, oh no!, say what?!, really?!
:(	Sad. I hope this one is not in the book.
:)	A smile.
:)\`\`\`\`	Drooling. If this is not in the book, It probably should have been.
:/	Perplexed, not totally satisfied or really happy, but acknowledged.
:P	Tongue in cheek, kidding.
;)	A wink and a smile.
;P	Kidding with a wink. Clearly, that's too much kidding. We won't be having that much kidding.

Ah-Ha	A moment of realization. Like when you're the last one to find out your charisma is irresistible. Aaahh-Haaaa. :))
Bitch-fest	The negative ranting of the unconscious mind. The kind of ranting that does not want solace or a solution. It's the rant that keeps on ranting just for the rant of it. ....shut up already! : o
Bla, bla, bla	The inane, insane droning of the unconscious thinking mind.
Bodhisattva	Someone who's willing to forgo personal Enlightenment, to teach others about it.
Consciousness	The container in which all is held. The seed of all manifestation. The Awareness behind the thinking. I Am, therefore I am able to think.
Crazy Train	When you are totally unconscious and submerged inside the ramblings of your thinking mind, like an out of control runaway train, only with crazy people on it.

Gatekeeper	A Present Gatekeeper has the power to let Truth (happiness) in and the power to boot untruth (unhappiness) out. "Beat it, get outta here!"
Hmmm	That's the sound thinking makes. : o
Isness	The natural, naked truth of a situation. It is actuality in its true form, before the mind discombobulates it.
Kensho	Moments of enlightenment. You're doing something good! :P
lol	Laugh out loud.
Onion	A representation for a complex situation comprised of many layers of ideas and emotions, with a crux or core issue. Duh. :P
Pointer	Someone who points to Awakening, and how to get there.

Pond, the	An analogy of the thinking mind, the id, personality, ego, the wack-a-do in your head that's been, to your surprise, unconscious and lying most of the time. : o
Prince	Shhhh. When u whisper his name, u can hear the angels sing. :) His name is Prince, and he is funky. His name is Prince - the one and only. :)
Satori	Moments of enlightenment. You're still doing something good! :P
Torrance, Jack	The disturbing character played by Jack Nicholson in the movie The Shinning. Great, now I can't get that face out of my head. :/
Unconsciousness	Being submersed in and believing my thoughts rather than observing and recognizing them. It's like amnesia, with the continual potential for pain and suffering. : o
Vision Board	A board or piece of paper with images of all the ridiculously expensive, and wonderfully outrageous stuff you want. Stuff like a billion dollars and a Dodo bird. BTW, they're lots of fun - the vision boards, not the Dodo bird.

Wack-a-do   Come on, really?

What?   That's you, your surprised reaction
                       to some of my comments. Or
                       sometimes it's me, intuitively
                       acknowledging when you have a
                       question. ...Your welcome. :)

SHIFT HAPPENS
A LAYPERSONS GUIDE TO AWAKENING

written and illustrated by
GINA CHARLES

Distribution:

Print

Digital Download

Audio Book

Please check the website for more information.

Visit the website and connect with me online:

www.ginacharles.com

---

www.ingramcontent.com/pod-product-compliance
Lightning Source LLC
Chambersburg PA
CBHW060939040426

42445CB00011B/928